Change My Heart, Oh God

INTEGRITY HOUSE™

An imprint of Integrity Publishers

CHANGE MY HEART, OH GOD

Published by Integrity Publishers, a division of Integrity Media, Inc., 5250 Virginia Way, Suite 110, Brentwood, TN 37027.

Integrity House is a registered trademark of Integrity Media, Inc.

HELPING PEOPLE WORLDWIDE EXPERIENCE *the* MANIFEST PRESENCE *of* GOD.

Produced with the assistance of The Livingstone Corporation (www.Livingstone Corp.com). Project staff includes David Veerman, Linda Taylor, Ashley Taylor.

Interior design/Cover design by The Office of Bill Chiaravalle | www.officeofbc.com

Library of Congress Cataloging-in-Publication Data

Fielding, Carol Chaffee.
   Change my heart, oh God : daily devotionals from the greatest praise and worship songs of all time : devotions / written by Carol Chaffee Fielding.
   p. cm.
   ISBN 1-59145-087-X
   1. Devotional calendars. I. Title.
BV4811.F54 2003
242'.2—dc21   2003009944

Printed and bound in Belgium

03 04 05 06 07 SPL 9 8 7 6 5 4 3 2 1

Table of Contents

INTRODUCTION

Our awesome God loves us so much! In His grace and mercy, He reaches down to touch our lives and change our hearts. Deep down, that is what we desire. No matter what may be happening in the uncertain world around us, we want our hearts changed—filled with His joy, His peace, His love. We want to hope in the future. We want to truly love and serve others. In short, we want to be more like Him.

Change My Heart, Oh God is a daily devotional that will guide you through the words of many songs of praise and worship. Read the words and meditate on them. Perhaps you will find that your own feelings are being expressed—but in a new and exciting way. Close your eyes. Let the songs remind you of all that God has done in your heart. Let them express the deepest desires of your heart. Let them fill your heart to overflowing with love for your Savior and Lord.

Worship and praise can work a change in your heart. Who hasn't sat in a church service at one time or another and felt the glorious presence of God through a song? Sometimes it's the words that speak directly to your need; sometimes it's the glorious music that seems to draw you right into heaven's throne room. You sense that God is speaking. You want Him to change your heart. You want to be more like Him.

This book gives you ninety days of devotional thoughts. Read the words of the songs—sing them if you know the tune. Let the lyrics sink into your being. Read the devotional, written to give you something to think about and something to take with you as you move into your day. Study the accompanying Bible verse. Then talk to God in prayer.

May God bless you as you come to Him seeking to have your heart changed. Then you can sing with the psalmist, "My heart is steadfast, O God, my heart is steadfast; I will sing and make music" (Psalm 57:7).

Change My Heart, Oh God

Change my heart, oh God;
Make it ever true.
Change my heart, oh God;
May I be like You.

You are the Potter,
I am the clay,
Mold me and make me,
This is what I pray.

—EDDIE ESPINOSA

The work of a potter is serious business. If you've ever watched a potter at the wheel, you know the time it takes to create a clay jar, bowl, or pot. The clay must be prepared properly, first removing all impurities that would cause the vessel to crack under the heat of firing. The potter works the clay, cutting, pounding, and kneading in order to remove bubbles. Then he shapes the vessel, working deftly with his hands as the wheel spins. Finally, the vessel is fired to nearly twenty-four hundred degrees. All of this is done to produce a strong, usable, high-quality vessel.

How blessed we are to have the Master Potter molding us! He prepares us with His Word and removes all our impurities through His loving forgiveness. He makes us stronger as we endure the cutting, pounding, and kneading of trials and difficult circumstances.

Then a most remarkable change takes place. He takes us, ugly lumps of muddy clay that we are, and forms us into items of great beauty and usability. He shapes us into exactly what He wants us to be, then He burns His love into our souls.

Undergoing the process of being molded may not always be comfortable, but the end result is always worth it. Ask God to mold you and make you, for when He does, He makes you more like Himself.

Yet, O LORD, you are our Father. We are the clay, you are the potter; we are all the work of your hand.

ISAIAH 64:8

PRAYER

Repeat aloud the first four lines of the song. With a willingness to change, pray that God will change your heart and make it ever true to Him.

How Great, How Glorious

How great, how glorious,
How wondrous are Your ways,
You reign victorious lifted high
upon our praise.
You are enthroned on the praises
of Your people,
God with us, You are called Emmanuel.
God is our strength, God is our refuge,
And a very present help in time of trouble.
You're great, You're glorious,
How excellent is Your name.
You reign victorious lifted high
upon our praise.
You're great and greatly to be praised.

—DON MOEN AND MARTIN J. NYSTROM

hy do we praise? What causes us to lift our voices and worship God? From the beginning of time, all of humanity has had reasons to praise almighty God—from the creation of the heavens and the earth to the promise of new heavens and a new earth, from the gift of the Promised Land to the gift of salvation through the promised Emmanuel. Indeed, God is great and greatly to be praised!

How should we praise the Lord? How can we lift Him high upon our praise? We do that when we live to glorify Him, when we thank Him, when we use our gifts to serve Him. How many ways can we praise God? As many ways as we can imagine! David played his harp; Solomon ruled with wisdom; Paul wrote letters to churches; C. S. Lewis wrote great literary works; Charles Colson ministered in prison; Fanny Crosby composed hymns; Billy Graham preached to hundreds of thousands. But most important, we praise God when we enthrone Him in our lives—making everything we do a sacrifice of praise to Him.

God is great, glorious, and excellent. May our lives reflect His power and glory. May His praise be ever on our lips, for He is greatly to be praised!

Through Jesus, therefore, let us continually offer to God a sacrifice of praise—the fruit of lips that confess his name.

HEBREWS 13:15

PRAYER

Thank God for the great and glorious things He has done in your life. Praise Him for His daily blessings and guidance.

Jehovah-Jireh

Jehovah-Jireh my provider,
His grace is sufficient for me, for me, for me.
Jehovah-Jireh my provider,
His grace is sufficient for me.
My God shall supply all my needs
According to His riches in glory,
He will give His angels charge over me.
Jehovah-Jireh cares for me, for me, for me,
Jehovah-Jireh cares for me.

—MERLA WATSON

*D*o we truly believe that Jehovah-Jireh (which means "God our provider") cares for us? We may say that we trust Him, but . . .

So we work hard to save the money to buy a car, a house, and a quality education for our children. While such planning is not bad, it can become a problem if having our needs met is not enough and we feel that we must assuage all our desires as well.

God our Provider promises to supply all our needs. What are our needs? Food, clothing, and shelter are life's most basic needs. Does God provide these? We would probably have to answer that yes, indeed, we have food, clothing, and shelter—that God has provided for us. While He may not have met all our desires, He has indeed met all our needs.

But even more important than Jehovah-Jireh's provision for our physical needs is His provision for our spiritual need. He has provided grace that is sufficient to fill the longing in our hearts for God. It is by His grace alone that we can come to Him.

Unlike the trendy clothes, gourmet food, and fancy house, grace is free and it is eternal. We don't have to earn it. We can't purchase it. It is offered as a gift. And it is ours—forever.

But he said to me, "My grace is sufficient for you, for my power is made perfect in weakness."

2 CORINTHIANS 12:9

PRAYER

Thank the Lord for His gift of grace and ask Him to help you share your faith and your abundance with others.

Send It On Down

Send it on down, send it on down,
Lord, let the Holy Ghost come on down.
Lord, we're Your children
And we are asking for You to send the fire.
Our hearts are hungry, our spirits are thirsty,
We need to feel Your fire.
Just like the prophet, he said it would be
In the last days an outpouring we'd see.
Yes we are waiting, we're anticipating,
Lord, won't You send the Holy Ghost down.
Heavenly Father, hear our call,
Let Your Holy Spirit fall.
Send down the power, let it fall like rain
As we lift our praises to Your name.

—GERON DAVIS

*I*magine how the disciples must have felt at the day of Pentecost when the Holy Spirit literally came down upon them! Picture that powerful scene: God made His presence known with the blowing of a violent wind and tongues of fire (Acts 2:2–3). Those who had been touched began to speak in other languages, proclaiming the wonders of God.

The disciples had been on a roller coaster of emotions. They had seen Jesus heal the sick, raise the dead, die on a cross, rise from the dead, and ascend to heaven—only to leave them to carry on His work. Now they were expected to go into all the world, preaching the gospel. How were they to accomplish this task? How could God have left such a responsibility in their inexperienced hands? He could do it because He knew, when the Holy Spirit came down upon them, they could change the world. So God sent the Spirit down—and the world has never been the same.

Do you feel weak? Incapable of running the race set before you? You already have the Holy Spirit, but sometimes you need to be re-ignited with fresh fire; sometimes you need to be refreshed with power sent down like rain into your soul. Ask God to send it on down! At your request, He will pour down His power and refreshment to help you do whatever He has called you to do, no matter how weak you feel.

But you will receive power when the Holy Spirit comes on you.

A C T S   1 : 8

P R A Y E R

God promises extraordinary results when we ask for His power. Ask Him to reignite your fire and to refresh your spirit so that you can do His work in your world.

The Solid Rock

You're the solid rock on which I stand,
You are the Christ the Risen Lamb.
The Lamb Who sits upon the throne
With tender mercies for His own.
I praise You now, O Risen Lamb,
You're the solid rock on which I stand.
Day after day, I will praise Your name,
In everything I will be glad.
For by Your grace You saved me
And on Your every Word I will depend.

—DON HARRIS

*I*f you have ever stood on a sandy beach as the waves lapped at your feet, you know that the longer you remain, the further your feet sink into the shifting sands. Eventually, you'll be up to your ankles! On a rocky coastline in Maine, however, you can stand on the shore with wave after wave rushing over your feet and you won't sink at all. You stand firm on the strength of the boulders beneath you.

Shifting sands don't make a very good foundation—for our feet or for our faith. We need solid rock—strong and unchanging. Like the wise man who built his house upon a rock (Luke 6:48), we can rest secure in building our faith upon the firm foundation of Jesus Christ. When the winds of change blow and the waves of uncertainty rush over us, we can cling to the immovable, unchanging love of Jesus.

For this we have reason to praise. Christ is the solid rock on which we stand. We can depend upon His words, trust in His tender mercies, and praise Him day after day for the grace that has saved us. Praise the risen Lamb and in everything be glad. Our foundation is firm; our salvation is sure. Praise His name!

Consequently, you are no longer foreigners and aliens, but fellow citizens with God's people and members of God's household, built on the foundation of the apostles and prophets, with Christ Jesus himself as the chief cornerstone.

Ephesians 2:19–20

PRAYER

Thank the Lord for His strength, support, mercy, and unchanging love. Thank Him for the gift of His Son, Jesus, the solid rock on which you can stand secure no matter what the waves of circumstance bring your way.

D A Y   6

As for Me and My House

As for me and my house, we will
serve the Lord.
We have counted the cost, we have
made the choice,
We will follow our God and obey His voice.
From this day and for the rest of our lives,
We will serve the Lord.
We will not bow to another god,
We will have no other gods but You,
We will not serve two masters,
We surrender our lives to You.

—TOM BROOKS, DON HARRIS, MARTIN J. NYSTROM

*W*hat better example to your family than proclaiming and living the words, "As for me and my house, we will serve the Lord"? Most people, especially children, learn by example. When you take a stand for God, not only proclaiming His lordship over your life but also living it to the fullest, others will learn to do the same.

However, sometimes we run into trouble. Many daily activities tend to take priority over our lives: the quest for a promotion at work, striving to be a top athlete, or pursuing excellence in academics. While all are noble causes, when we slip into seeking to control our lives in order to reach our goals, we rebel against the lordship of Jesus Christ and we are serving other gods.

God knows the desires of our hearts. He knows our needs and our wants. He wants us to be happy, but He also knows what is best for us. When we decide to serve the Lord, we open ourselves to His blessings. When we surrender ourselves to His will, we choose to let Him be Lord of our lives—every part of them.

Have you made the choice? Who will you and your family serve? Can you say with confidence, "As for me and my house, we will serve the Lord"? How will you make that a reality in your home today?

And if it seems evil to you to serve the LORD, choose for yourselves this day whom you will serve. . . . But as for me and my house, we will serve the LORD.

JOSHUA 24:15 (NKJV)

PRAYER

As a family, pray that God will guide you and bless you as you choose to serve Him together.

13

The Family Prayer Song

Come and fill our homes with Your presence,

You alone are worthy of our reverence.

As for me and my house, we will

serve the Lord.

Lord we vow to live holy,

Bowing our knees to You only,

Staying together, praying together,

Any storm we can weather

Trusting in God's Word.

We need each other,

Fathers and mothers, sisters and brothers,

In harmony and love.

—MORRIS CHAPMAN

*T*ry this experiment: Go outside and pick up a twig. Grasping each end, bend the twig. It bends easily, doesn't it? It may even break. Now, pick up four or five twigs. Holding them together in a bunch, try to bend them. Not as easy, is it?

The same principle holds true for families. When all in a family are united in harmony—staying together, praying together—the storms of life may shake us, but they won't break us.

How much more powerful, then, the family who stands together in the Lord! In Matthew 18:20, Jesus promised, "Where two or three come together in my name, there am I with them." When we invite Jesus to fill our home with His presence, we will be blessed to find harmony and love which could never exist without Him.

We need one another in every way—praying before meals, doing devotions daily, attending church services as a family, working in the yard, and watching TV together. The family that is unified, that vows to live according to God's Word, will weather the storms of life and be stronger for the journey.

How good and pleasant it is when brothers live together in unity!

PSALM 133:1

PRAYER

Make a commitment that your family will live in unity, working together that you may be a positive example in the world. Ask the Lord to help you as you work toward this goal each day.

Purify My Heart

Purify my heart,

Touch me with Your cleansing fire.

Take me to the cross,

Your holiness is my desire.

Breathe Your life in me,

Kindle the love that flows from Your throne.

O purify my heart,

Purify my heart.

—JEFF NELSON

*A*s gold is heated to a temperature of nearly two thousand degrees, impurities rise to the surface, making them easy to remove. When the remaining gold is cooled, the result is a refined, pure, high-quality gold; it is precious and valuable.

We are precious to God and valuable enough for Him to have sent His Son to earth to suffer death on a cross. His death served as a payment for us to spend eternity in heaven with Him. As Christians, we know we have been cleansed of our sins, yet we constantly face the struggle with our sin natures. What can we do? We can continually ask for God's cleansing fire. Each day, we can ask Him to purify us.

There is no need to fear the Refiner's fire. Isaiah submitted to the cleansing fire of a burning coal upon his lips (Isaiah 6:5–8). A cleansing process was necessary before Isaiah could fulfill his purpose as a prophet of God. God's method of purification may not be comfortable. It may force us to wrestle with issues buried deep within our hearts. It may even be painful. But submission to the cleansing fire of God will allow us to be made pure in His sight.

And that is all we could ever desire.

These trials are only to test your faith, to show that it is strong and pure. It is being tested as fire tests and purifies gold—and your faith is far more precious to God than mere gold.

1 PETER 1:7 (NLT)

PRAYER

Pray that the Lord will reveal your weaknesses, forgive your sins, and purify your heart as you lean on His everlasting love.

He Knows My Name

I have a Maker
He formed my heart
Before even time began
My life was in His hand.
He knows my name,
He knows my every thought,
He sees each tear that falls
And hears me when I call.
I have a Father,
He calls me His own,
He'll never leave me
No matter where I go.

—TOMMY WALKER

On a transcontinental flight, cruising along at thirty thousand feet, everything on the ground looks miniscule. Mountains appear as bumps in the landscape, roads are thin ribbons, and houses and people are indistinguishable.

How awesome it is to know that God, looking down from His lofty throne, knows your name. He sees your struggles and pain; He hears every prayer and longing of your heart. He sees each tear that falls. You aren't just a tiny dot in the landscape on planet earth. You have a Maker and Redeemer. You have worth. You are loved.

Not only does He know you, He has a purpose for your life. He calls you His own. He never leaves you; He walks with you wherever you go. Each day, you interact with dozens of people who don't know you and may never interact with you again—from the telemarketer to the cashier at the grocery store. How you respond to others is a witness to your relationship with God. When your life displays the fruit of the Spirit (love, joy, peace, patience, goodness, faithfulness, gentleness, and self-control), you show to whom you belong.

Does how you live bring your Father great pleasure?

I knew you before I formed you in your mother's womb. Before you were born I set you apart and appointed you as my spokesman to the world.

JEREMIAH 1:5 (NLT)

PRAYER

Thank the Lord for being the One who knows you better than you know yourself, and for recognizing you by name when you come to His throne in prayer.

I Was Glad

I was glad when they said unto me,
Let us go into Your house, oh Lord.
No greater love than to be in this place
To lift my voice and sing Your praise.

Here we are, in Your courts we stand
With our hearts and hands upraised.
Here we are by the blood of the Lamb.
By Your grace we come
And by Your grace we stand.

To lift my voice and sing Your praise,
To lift my voice and sing Your praise.

—GERRIT GUSTAFSON AND DON MOEN

*J*esus Christ is your Savior and Friend, but He is also your sovereign Lord. When you approach Him, whether in a house of worship or on your knees at your bedside, you must show reverence and respect.

When you step into your church, how do you feel? What do you see? What brings you to the realization that you are in His house, His courts? Do you ever contemplate the fact that you are there by His grace alone? When you praise with a pure and contrite heart, reverently stepping into God's presence, you can meet Him anywhere, transforming an elevator, your backyard, or even your car into a place where you are in His awesome presence.

When you come to God in worship, you come knowing that you are worthy of His blessings only because of His undeserved grace. In Psalm 28, David calls out, "Hear my cry for mercy as I call to you for help, as I lift my hands toward your Most Holy Place." You can receive all God has to offer when you reverently approach the throne of grace with heart and hands open to the blessings of the Most Holy Lord.

I was glad when they said unto me, Let us go into the house of the Lord.

PSALM 122:1 (KJV)

PRAYER

Approach the Lord in prayer with respect and reverence, knowing that wherever you meet Him is holy ground. Ask Him to remind you each day of His holiness.

You Alone Are Holy

Can you hear creation yearning

Longing to worship His name?

Together in all adoration, I join them to proclaim.

Can you hear the angels singing,

In the presence of the King?

My heart cries out to be with them

As I fall on my knees and sing.

For You alone are holy, You are worthy to be praised.

You alone are holy, I offer up myself to You,

For it's the least that I can do for You.

To live my life in Your presence,

To hide in the wings of Your grace,

To drink from Your fountain of mercy,

I hunger and see Your face.

—Greg Gulley and Lenny LeBlanc

*G*od alone is holy! The only being in the universe worthy of our praise is our Lord Jesus Christ. If we are silent, the whole of creation will rise and shout praises to the Creator, Most Holy God. In Jerusalem, the Pharisees told Jesus to tell the crowds to be quiet, to cease their praises. Jesus replied, "If they keep quiet, the stones will cry out" (Luke 19:40).

In the Book of Revelation, John is blessed to see the holiness of Jesus revealed to him in a dream. The heavenly beings never cease in saying, "Holy, holy, holy is the Lord God Almighty, who was, and is, and is to come" (Revelation 4:8). How wonderful to know that we will someday join with the angels in proclaiming the holiness of God face to face with our Savior!

Until then, we can live life in His presence, worshiping and offering our hearts to Him. He loves us so much! Loving Him in return is what He desires; as the song says, "it's the least we can do." And when we live in praise we find great blessings. He will keep us safe in the shadow of His wings (Psalm 17:8), watching over us as a mother hen would protect her young by spreading her wings over them. He allows us to drink from the "fountain of life" (Psalm 36:9).

Offer yourself to the Holy One. You will not be disappointed.

Let them praise the name of the LORD, for His name alone is exalted; His glory is above the earth and heaven.

PSALM 148:13 (NKJV)

PRAYER

Fall on your knees and worship the Lord. Thank Him for His mercy and protection. Proclaim His holiness, for He is worthy to be praised!

No Eye Has Seen

No eye has seen, no ear has heard,
No mind has conceived what the
Lord has prepared.
But by His Spirit He has revealed
His plan to those who love Him.
We've been held by His everlasting love,
Led with loving kindness by His hand.
We have hope for the future yet to come
In time we'll understand the mystery
of His plan.

—PAUL BALOCHE AND ED KERR

Even in your wildest daydreams you could never imagine what eternity with Jesus will be like. The inkling John gives us in Revelation 21 only serves to heighten the mystery and our anticipation. John describes a city made of precious and rare jewels, with gold so pure it is transparent.

Because we are all unique in our perception of written descriptions, each one of us will picture something different in our mind's eye. You may have a detailed image in your mind of what you think heaven will be like. When you finally arrive there, no matter what your preconceived ideas, you will not be disappointed.

Until then, live each day seeking to know what God has planned for you right here, right now. He has much in store for your life. When you pray daily for His guidance, the Holy Spirit will lead you. The Old Testament prophet Jeremiah encouraged God's people by telling them God's promise: "I know the plans I have for you . . . plans to prosper you and not to harm you, plans to give you a hope and a future" (Jeremiah 29:11). Just as God was with the ancient peoples, He is with you today, leading you all the way. His plans are good, bringing hope for the future in this life and beyond. God has prepared something wonderful just for you!

No eye has seen, no ear has heard, no mind has conceived what God has prepared for those who love him.

1 CORINTHIANS 2:9

PRAYER

Think about heaven—the place God has prepared for you. Thank Him for the plans He has for you, for giving you hope for this life and life with Him for eternity.

I Belong to Jesus

Satan goes around like a roaring lion seeking
whom he may devour,
But he has been defeated so I'm testifyin'
By the blood of Jesus, he lost his pow'r.
Christ was lifted up with my sin upon Him,
His life and blood came flowing down.
So hear me, I'm declaring Jesus Christ is Lord.
I'm taking back His holy ground.
I belong to Jesus, I belong to Him, I belong to
Jesus free from sin.
All sin nailed to the cross and the
Lamb's blood flowing
Meant victory was sealed that day.
When Satan saw the blood, he knew that Christ
had won it
And he knew that Sunday was on its way.

—Dennis Jernigan

e all want to feel like we belong. We are conditioned from birth to need to belong to someone. We experience belonging in our families, with our friends, with a spouse, in our church. And although each of these relationships fills that need to a certain extent, we can never feel truly satisfied, we can never truly belong, until we belong to Jesus.

The reason is simple. Life changes. We grow up and move out of our parents' home. Some of our friends move away. We may lose our spouse to divorce or death. There is only One person to whom we can belong forever—in this life and beyond. If we've made the choice to belong to Him, He will never leave us.

In fact, His life and death were meant for the purpose of giving all people a chance to belong to the family of God. He took your sin upon Himself as He was nailed to the cross. He bought your freedom with His blood. This is an intense, all-encompassing freedom—freedom from Satan's power, from sin and destruction, freedom to live your life in the joy of belonging to Christ the King. Rejoice that you can proclaim "I belong to Jesus!" now, and forever.

He destined us for adoption as his children through Jesus Christ. . . . In him we have redemption through his blood, the forgiveness of our trespasses, according to the riches of his grace.

EPHESIANS 1:5, 7 (NRSV)

PRAYER

Recognize how good it feels when you repeat "I belong to Jesus" again and again. Thank the Lord for setting you free and allowing you to belong to Him. Ask Him to help you share your joy and freedom with others.

I Love Your Grace

I love Your grace, I love Your mercy,
I love the way You help me when I call.
I love the truth, I love the power of
Your name,
But You know I love Your presence
most of all.
My soul takes refuge in the shadow of
Your wings,
Close to You is where I want to be.
You are my strength,
You are my God, You are my King
All I want is what You want for me.

—RICK FOUNDS

*W*hy do you love Jesus? What causes you to rely on Him and trust Him enough to give your heart and soul to Him?

Those trying, stressful days when everything seems to be closing in on you sometimes feel like more than you can handle. You fall into bed at night wondering how you made it through. Then you remember that you spent time with God at the start of the day. You recall how, when the pressure was on, you called out to God for strength and serenity. And in the quiet of your heart, it hits you: He was there with you all day long!

That's why you love Jesus. All you had to do was ask, and His mercy was poured out upon you; grace was freely given. Now His presence surrounds you day by day. He is there, listening to your prayers and answering when you call. He is there, lending His strength. He is there, providing a place of refuge from the stormy day. Praise Him, for He is there.

Have mercy on me, O God, have mercy on me, for in you my soul takes refuge. I will take refuge in the shadow of your wings until the disaster has passed.

PSALM 57:1

PRAYER

Think about the times when you felt overwhelmed. Now think of the ways in which God made His presence known to you through those stressful periods. Tell Him that all you want is what He wants for you.

29

You Alone

You are the peace that guards my heart,
My help in time of need.
You are the hope that leads me on
And brings me to my knees.
For there I find You waiting,
And there I find release.
So with all my heart I'll worship
And unto You I'll sing.
For You alone deserve all glory,
For You alone deserve all praise.
Father, we worship and adore You,
Father, we long to see Your face.
For You alone deserve all glory,
For You alone deserve all praise.
Father, we love You,
And we worship You this day.

—DON HARRIS

While working at a small, non-religious private school, a Christian teacher handled the stresses of the environment with a positive attitude and a calmness not exhibited by his co-workers. Because of the way he responded to volatile situations, he was respected by his students. They went to him with their problems and concerns, and listened intently to his advice.

One day, another faculty member asked him, "How do you do it? How do you maintain your positive outlook with everything we go through each day?"

His answer was simple: "Jesus." He told of his daily quiet time in which he asked God for strength and wisdom for what lay ahead. He told of the peace he receives when, in his uncertainty, he relies on Jesus. And he told his co-worker how she could also find this peace and the strength to handle the day.

Where do you go when you need peace, help, and hope? How do you face each day with all of its uncertainty? When you go to Jesus in prayer, He will answer your call. He will not leave you to go it alone— He can, and will, carry it all.

When I pray, you answer me; you encourage me by giving me the strength I need.
PSALM 138:3 (NLT)

PRAYER

Go to the Lord and ask for His peace and wisdom. Ask Him to help you live in a way that, by your example, others will want to know Him too.

Heaven Is in My Heart/God Is So Good/Amazing Grace

Heaven is in my heart, the Kingdom of our God is here.

Heaven is in my heart, the presence of His majesty.

Heaven is in my heart and in His presence joy abounds.

Heaven is in my heart, the light of holiness surrounds.

We are temples for His throne, heaven is in my heart

And Christ is the foundation stone, heaven is in my heart.

He will return to take us home, heaven is in my heart.

The Spirit and the bride say come, heaven is in my heart.

God is so good, He's so good to me.

Amazing grace, how sweet the sound that saved
a wretch like me,
I once was lost but now I'm found,
was blind but now I see.

—GRAHAM KENDRICK / JOHN NEWTON

*H*eaven: A most spectacular and beautiful place where there will be no night, and yet no need for sun to light the day (Revelation 21:23; 22:5). The reason for this phenomenon? The presence of Jesus!

When you invited Jesus to live in your heart, you invited an everlasting light. The presence of His majesty drove out the darkness of fear and doubt and replaced it with joy. His holy light, residing on the throne of your heart, becomes a symbol of heaven within you. God is so good to you that He gave His only Son as a sacrifice for your sins. That sacrifice cleansed your heart and made it a suitable place for God to dwell. Now heaven is indeed in your heart.

Yes, Christ saved your soul when you accepted His gift of grace. You probably know the words by heart, but read them once again: "Amazing grace, how sweet the sound, that saved a wretch like me." Your heart was once in darkness, but God, in His goodness, gave you a second chance. When you asked Him to enter your life and make your heart His temple, your blindness was removed and you saw the light of His presence. Hallelujah for His great love!

But because of his great love for us, God, who is rich in mercy, made us alive with Christ even when we were dead in transgressions—it is by grace you have been saved.

EPHESIANS 2:4–5

PRAYER

Thank the Lord for His goodness, His willingness to bring His everlasting light into the darkness of your heart and, most of all, for His sacrifice that cleansed you from sin.

Blessed Be the Rock

Blessed be the rock of my salvation.
Blessed be the rock of my salvation.
For the Lord is on my side
And He's made His victory mine.
Blessed be the rock of my salvation.

—DANIEL GARDNER

When Jesus entered the city of Jerusalem riding on a donkey, the people shouted their praises, "Blessed is the king who comes in the name of the Lord!" (Luke 19:38). They were praising God for giving them someone whom, they thought, would be their king—a man who would become ruler of Israel. They had the wrong idea.

Jesus came not to overthrow the government, but to overthrow the powers of hell and their ruler. He came to rule in people's hearts. He came to be a cornerstone on which the church would build its faith— He came to be the rock of our salvation.

Blessed be the rock of our salvation! This mighty rock provides a solid place on which to build our faith as we read the Scriptures and learn more about Him every day. His great love saved us—giving us victory over anger, doubt, fear, and death because He is on our side. For that, He is worthy of our praise.

Blessed be the rock!

The LORD is my rock, my fortress and my deliverer; my God is my rock, in whom I take refuge, my shield and the horn of my salvation. He is my stronghold, my refuge and my savior.

2 SAMUEL 22:2−3

PRAYER

Ask God to remind you every day to cling to the rock, to stand firm in your faith, and be an example for others to follow.

He Is the King

He is the King, He is the Lord,
He is the One Who delivers me.
Hail to the King, hail to the Lord,
Hail to the One Who delivers me.
Jesus, strong and mighty King
Ruling over all the kingdoms of this world.
Lift your voice to Him and sing,
He is Lord of everything.
He is the King of kings.

—TOM EWING, DON MOEN, AND REV. JOHN STOCKER

In the Old Testament, you'll find that the Israelites were often engaged in battle—most of the time for land or for freedom from oppressors. They gave credit to the Lord for their victories, for delivering them from the hand of their enemies. In Psalm 24, the priests inside the temple would ask, "Who is this King of glory?" The people outside would respond, "The LORD strong and mighty, the LORD mighty in battle." Then the gates to the temple would be opened and the people would enter to worship and offer their thanksgiving to God.

Today, you can give credit to the Lord for your victories. The battles may be large (your triumph over an unhealthy or self-destructive habit) or small (you didn't lose your temper during the traffic jam). He is the one who delivers you in every situation. He provides patience or self-control when you need it the most. He hears and answers every time you call. He is the King, He is the Lord. Praise His name, the name of Jesus, the strong and mighty ruler of the kingdoms of this world—and of the kingdom of your heart.

Who is this King of glory? The LORD strong and mighty, the LORD mighty in battle.

PSALM 24:8

PRAYER

Praise the Lord for His victory in your heart. Thank Him for providing the strength needed to help you overcome your personal battles.

Yes Lord Yes

And my answer will be yes, Lord, yes,

Lord, I give You all the glory for all You've given me.

You have filled my life until I overflowed.

All I have is Yours to use any way You choose.

You are Lord of all, so how can I say no?

I'll say yes, Lord, yes to Your will and to Your way.

I'll say yes, Lord, yes, I will trust You and obey.

When Your Spirit speaks to me with my

whole heart I'll agree

And my answer will be yes, Lord, yes.

If I never knew the fullness of living in Your will,

I would never know how rich my life could be.

Lord my willingness to serve is the least that You deserve

For the blessings You have showered over me.

—LYNN KEESECKER

*O*bedience. Now there's a word that meets resistance! Due to our nature, we often balk at authority, at the very thought of doing what we're told.

Jesus, in the Garden of Gethsemane, faced the question of obedience. He knew what lay ahead if He followed God's plan for Him. He would be mocked, His friends would desert Him, He would be whipped, nailed to a cross, die by suffocation, and endure total separation from God. He even asked God if He could get out of the whole situation, saying, "Father, if you are willing, take this cup from me." But in the same breath, He reaffirmed His commitment to obedience, "Yet not my will, but yours be done" (Luke 22:42).

Jesus obeyed God's plan—He answered with a "yes" that resulted in salvation for all who believe. After all He's done for you, how, then, could you tell God "no" when He asks you for your obedience?

You can't always know or even predict the outcome of your obedience to God. But when you respond with a "Yes, Lord, yes," you can be assured He will use you for His glory. And you also can be assured that your life will be richer and fuller than you could ever have imagined.

Those who obey his commands live in him, and he in them. And this is how we know that he lives in us: We know it by the Spirit he gave us.

1 JOHN 3:24

PRAYER

Think about some areas in your life in which you need to be obedient to God. Commit yourself to obedience to God's Word, and reaffirm this by saying "Yes, Lord, yes" to each area in need.

Jesus Is the Answer

Jesus is the answer for the world today.

Above Him there's no other 'cause Jesus is the way.

If you have some questions in the corners of your mind,

And traces of discouragement, and

peace you cannot find.

Reflections of your past seem to face you every day,

But this one thing I do know, that Jesus is the way.

I know you've got mountains that you think

you cannot climb.

I know your skies are dark, you think the

sun won't shine.

In case you don't know but the Word of God is true

And everything He's promised, He will do it for you.

—ANDRAE AND SANDRA CROUCH

*T*he world today has many religions to offer those who are searching for answers. You could choose to believe whatever makes you comfortable—from reincarnation here on earth to populating your own planet in the afterlife.

But no matter where you look, there is one truth to Christianity that no other religion can claim: God sent His Son Jesus to die for the sins of all mankind, and three days later, Jesus rose from the dead. Jesus provided the way for a sinful humanity to find God. Because of the Cross, you can have a loving, personal relationship with God. Jesus is alive today, listening to the desires of your heart and answering when you call out to Him.

Yes, Jesus is the answer. Do you have a question about the meaning of life? Jesus is the answer. Do you wonder about your future? Jesus is the answer. Are your skies dark? Are you facing a mountain you don't think you can climb? Jesus is the answer. He knows your discouragement and fear, and He will help you find peace. He brings light to your darkest night.

The risen Savior is your answer, and the answer for anyone in the world who chooses to believe!

Jesus said to him, "I am the way, the truth, and the life. No one comes to the Father except through Me."

JOHN 14:6 (NKJV)

PRAYER

Write down some questions you have about God. Ask Him to help you find the answers as you spend time each day in prayer and Bible study.

Jesus Loves Me /
O How He Loves You and Me

Jesus loves me, this I know,

for the Bible tells me so.

Little ones to Him belong,

they are weak but He is strong.

Yes, Jesus loves me. Yes, Jesus loves me.

Yes, Jesus loves me, the Bible tells me so.

O how He loves you and me.

O how He loves you and me.

He gave His life, what more could He give?

O how He loves you, O how He loves me,

O how He loves you and me.

—LENNART SJOEHOLM / KURT KAISER

*W*hen you listen to this song, do you recall when you were a child, innocently singing the words in Sunday school? You believed the words without question. "Of course Jesus loves me. The Bible tells me so!" Then, you grew up, and the childlike innocence evaporated.

At a Christian college, a student sat in her Biblical Literature class and asked, "How do we know Jesus loves us? How do we know the Bible is true?"

The professor replied, "You tell me. How do you know?"

The young coed responded that she didn't know. Her belief was based on what she had been taught as a child by her parents and her church. The wise professor explained that, like a nice house that needs a new foundation, she should keep in her heart everything she had been taught—she just needed to "jack up" the house and build a new foundation formed from the cement of her own prayer and study of God's Word. She did just that and, as a result, her faith was made stronger.

In your heart you know the truth—that Jesus loves you so much that He gave His life for you. Continue to strengthen the foundation and build the house of faith by learning more about Jesus and sharing your faith with others.

Does Jesus love you? Of course He does. The Bible tells you so!

For God so loved the world that he gave his one and only Son, that whoever believes in him shall not perish but have eternal life.

JOHN 3:16

PRAYER

Think about how much God loves you. Thank Him for sending His Son to save you, providing you with a firm foundation for your faith.

I See the Lord

I see the Lord seated on the throne exalted
And the train of His robe fills the temple
with glory
And the whole earth is filled,
And the whole earth is filled,
And the whole earth is filled with His glory.
Holy, holy, holy, holy,
Holy is the Lord.

—CHRIS FALSON

What a marvelous vision! Can you picture the image in your mind? Jesus on the throne, the train of His robe covering the whole floor of the temple. Such a sight of splendor and majesty would bring anyone to his knees, bowing before the King.

Such a vision came to the prophet Isaiah in the Old Testament, who saw the Lord seated on His throne, high and exalted. The apostle John in the New Testament also was invited to see God's throne in heaven and experience the worship there. "Day and night they never stop saying: 'Holy, holy, holy is the Lord God Almighty, who was, and is, and is to come'" (Revelation 4:8). They fall on their knees and lay their crowns before Him.

When you come before the Lord in prayer, begin by worshiping His holiness, His majesty, and His glory. Picture Him as your King, seated high and exalted on a throne with all the powers of heaven giving Him praise and adoration. Allow yourself to be in awe of this great and awesome Creator of the universe who made Himself approachable by sending His Son to become human and die for your sins. Then do as the Bible says, "Come boldly to the throne of our gracious God. There we will receive his mercy, and we will find grace to help us when we need it" (Hebrews 4:16 NLT).

In the year that King Uzziah died, I saw the Lord seated on a throne, high and exalted, and the train of his robe filled the temple.

ISAIAH 6:1

PRAYER

Out loud, repeat, "Holy, holy, holy, holy. Holy is the Lord." Praise God for His holiness and thank Him for His mercy.

Hear Our Praises

May our homes be filled with dancing,

May our streets be filled with joy,

May injustice bow to Jesus as the people

turn and pray.

From the mountains to the valleys,

Hear our praises rise to You,

From the heavens to the nations,

Hear our singing fill the air.

May our light shine in the darkness as we

walk before the cross,

May Your glory fill the whole earth as the

water o'er the seas.

—REUBEN MORGAN

*W*ith our finite human minds, we cannot begin to imagine the celebration that takes place in the kingdom of heaven every time a sinner surrenders to Jesus. And greater still will be the rejoicing when each sinner saved by grace enters the gates of heaven, welcomed by those who have gone before.

But for now, we can pray as Jesus taught us to pray—"Your kingdom come" (Matthew 6:10). But how is that possible? How could His kingdom come? What exactly are we praying for when we say that? We're praying both for revival and for His return. When Christians all over the world unite their hearts and voices in praise! When His people pray—alone by their bedside or as thousands of believers—He will be there. When we praise, our voices join the chorus of millions, rising to heaven. As a result, the glory of God will fill the earth and His people will dance for joy. The nations will hear the praise of God's people; we can be a light shining in the darkness.

You can make a difference for God right where you are—in your home, at work, on vacation. Lift praises to God and be a true example of joy.

Shout for joy to the LORD, all the earth. Worship the LORD with gladness; come before him with joyful songs.

PSALM 100:1-2

PRAYER

Worship the Lord with thanksgiving and praise. Let your heart rejoice and thank Him for the joy He has given to you. Ask Him to let your joy overflow to others today.

I Walk by Faith

I walk by faith, each step by faith,
To live by faith I put my trust in You.
Every step I take is a step of faith,
No weapon formed against me shall prosper
And every prayer I make is a prayer of faith.
If my God is for me, who can be against me?

—CHRIS FALSON

*C*an you tell the future? Sure, there are lots of people who *claim* they can tell you what job you will have, whom you will marry, how long you will live—some even claim to know the day and the hour that Jesus will return. One thing is certain: The future is in God's hands and only He knows what is in store for you.

This doesn't mean you can just sit back and not think about what is ahead. Plans should be made for your well-being and security. Goals should be set. You do need to look ahead to the coming years. What it does mean is that, when you place your faith in God's leading, you don't have to *worry* about what lies ahead. God will give you the ability to gain what you need; He will provide you with strength to survive in times of trouble; He will give you a heart big enough to hold the joys He has in store for you.

"Trust in the LORD with all your heart, and lean not on your own understanding; in all your ways acknowledge Him, and He shall direct your paths" (Proverbs 3:5–6 NKJV). When you walk by faith and live by faith, you can trust in God to guide you through your future and on into eternity.

For we walk by faith, not by sight.

2 CORINTHIANS 5:7 (NKJV)

PRAYER

Ask the Lord to strengthen your faith and to help you to rely upon His leading in your life.

Your Everlasting Love

Your everlasting love is higher, higher, higher
than the sky.
All the wonder of Your everlasting love
Is higher than the sky.
Your everlasting love is deeper, deeper, deeper
than the sea.
All the wonder of Your everlasting love
Is deeper than the sea.
Higher than the heavens above is the glory of
Your wonderful love.
I'm lost in the mystery of Your everlasting love.
Your everlasting love is reaching, reaching,
reaching out to me.
Oh the wonder of Your everlasting love
Is reaching out to me.

—BILL BATSTONE

The dictionary defines *everlasting* as "never coming to an end; lasting forever; eternal." What kind of love could be described in such a way? Only the love God has poured out upon those who believe in Him.

It is difficult to imagine a love that will never end. Human beings are certainly capable of great love, but the wonder of a love that will never end is beyond our comprehension. God loves you so much, He knew you in your mother's womb—He knows everything about you from your thoughts to the desires of your heart, even to the number of hairs on your head! He knows your past, and He has forgiven you.

"Greater love has no one than this, that he lay down his life for his friends" (John 15:13). Jesus loved us enough to die for us; as Christians, we need to show the same sacrificial love toward others. His wonderful love is higher than the sky and deeper than the sea. He holds us close and reaches out to us when we stray. He is always there to give us more and more—and the well of His love will never run dry! Praise Him for His everlasting love!

I have loved you with an everlasting love; I have drawn you with loving-kindness.

JEREMIAH 31:3

PRAYER

Think of someone to whom you can show love. Thank the Lord that His love reached out to you, then reach out to others with His wonderful love.

My God Reigns

There's nowhere else that I'd rather be
Than dancing with You as You sing over me.
There's nothing else that I'd rather do, Lord,
than to worship You.
So rejoice, be glad, rejoice oh my soul,
For the Lord your God, He reigns forevermore.
I rejoice for my God reigns.
So rejoice, be glad, your Father and your Friend
Is the Lord your God whose rule will never end.
I rejoice for my God reigns.
My God reigns and I dance the dance of praise.
My God reigns, with a shout I will proclaim.
My God reigns and I worship without shame.
My God reigns and I will rejoice
For my God reigns.

—DARRELL EVANS

"Blessed are those who have learned to acclaim you, who walk in the light of your presence, O LORD. They rejoice in your name all day long; they exult in your righteousness" (Psalm 89:15–16). There is no place more amazing than the presence of the Lord. In His presence we can become fully involved in praise, dancing and singing as He sings over us.

Just as a proud father exults in the triumphs and joys of his children, our Father in heaven celebrates over us. When we hit bumps in the road, when we struggle, just like a loving dad, He is there to pick us up, dust us off, and fortify our spirits with His strength. He reigns supreme forevermore—yet even in His glory, He still has the desire to be our Friend.

So rejoice and be glad in the Lord. Worship without shame. Release your heart and soul as the Lord sings over you! So dance, shout, rejoice. Your God reigns!

The LORD your God is with you, he is mighty to save. He will take great delight in you, he will quiet you with his love, he will rejoice over you with singing.

ZEPHANIAH 3:17

PRAYER

Read the words of the song out loud. Pray aloud and thank God for His presence in your life.

I Will Celebrate

I will celebrate, sing unto the Lord,

I will sing to Him a new song.

I will praise Him

For He has triumphed victoriously.

—RITA BALOCHE

*T*his song invites us to celebrate and to praise God, but sometimes we aren't sure how to go about doing that. One way to praise is with our voices. The song declares, "I will celebrate, sing unto the Lord." Through our sincere desire to praise God, we can lift our voices and sing.

Jesus came to save all people from sin and, one day, He will return to this world to gather His children unto Himself. Someday, we will see our Jesus, our Savior, face to face—and we will sing praises with the heavenly host! What an astounding reason to celebrate!

We believe God is great and we should not keep our joy to ourselves. What He has done for us is overwhelming and we must share our appreciation for His victory—over sin, over death, over our lives. Knowing what He did for us should strengthen our commitment to Him—and to sharing our joy.

Sing your praise to God that others might hear the celebration and be drawn to know the truth: that Jesus is the Savior! Celebrate His triumph and victory. Sing a new song to the Lord!

I will praise you, O Lord, among the nations; I will sing of you among the peoples. For great is your love, reaching to the heavens; your faithfulness reaches to the skies.

PSALM 57:9–10

PRAYER

Praise the Lord for giving you a song in your heart and a voice to lift in celebration of His great love.

That's Why We Praise Him

He came to live, live a perfect life.
He came to be the Living Word, our light.
He came to die so we'd be reconciled.
He came to rise to show His pow'r and might.
That's why we praise Him, that's why we sing,
That's why we offer Him our everything.
That's why we bow down and worship this King
'Cause He gave His everything.
He came to live, live again in us.
He came to be our conquering King and Friend.
He came to heal and show the lost ones His love.
He came to go prepare a place for us.

— Tommy Walker

We praise Jesus for everything His life on earth meant for us, and we praise Him for all He continues to do in our lives.

Our lives without Jesus were no better than slavery—to the ways of the world, to our own desires, and to the power of Satan. When we knelt down at the feet of Jesus and allowed Him to conquer our hearts, we were set free.

Jesus heals the lost and transforms those dead in their transgressions to be made alive in Him. Where we were once subject to evil, we are now raised up in glory, free to live in the joy of His mercy and truth. We had been separated from God, but now we can be called His children. We are shown mercy instead of wrath, joy instead of sorrow, eternal life instead of eternal separation and death. He continues to be our King and our Friend. He is preparing a place for us in heaven, where we will have the blessing of praising Him forever.

That's why we praise Him; that's why we sing! He gave Himself up for our salvation—that's why we offer Him our everything.

I have come as a light to shine in this dark world, so that all who put their trust in me will no longer remain in the darkness.

JOHN 12:46 (NLT)

PRAYER

Thank Jesus for dying for your sins that you might be reconciled to God. Offer Him all that you are that He may use you for His glory.

Jesus, Jesus

Jesus, Jesus, one touch of Your hand,
I am healed and I am whole.
Jesus, Jesus, one glimpse of Your face
Brings fire to my soul.
And Jesus I come beholding Your face,
I am changed from glory to glory
And now I see and now I know
One touch of Your life brings
glory to my soul.
Jesus, Jesus, from darkness to light,
My life overflows.
Jesus, Jesus, Your mercy and grace
Like a river flowing down.

—GEOFF BULLOCK

*S*he had been under the care of many doctors, but instead of getting better, she only became worse. When she heard about Jesus, she sought Him out and found Him in the midst of a crowd. Because her illness caused her to be considered "unclean," she assumed Jesus would not want to touch her. So she came up behind Him in the crowd and touched His cloak, thinking, "If I just touch his clothes, I will be healed." She was right. Immediately, she was freed from her suffering.

Jesus felt the power go from Him, so He asked who touched His clothes. The woman, trembling in fear, admitted what she had done. To her surprise, Jesus replied, "Daughter, your faith has healed you. Go in peace" (Mark 5:25–34).

In times of desperation and pain, we can reach out to Him and He will respond to our faith and bless us beyond measure. When we look to Him to heal our brokenness and sorrow, we understand the real Jesus—the One who came not only to help us in this life, but to make a place for us in eternity.

So put your faith into action. Reach up to God. One touch of His hand brings healing to your hurting soul. One touch of His life brings glory so that your life will overflow.

And we, who with unveiled faces all reflect the Lord's glory, are being transformed into his likeness with ever-increasing glory, which comes from the Lord, who is the Spirit.

2 CORINTHIANS 3:18

PRAYER

Ask the Lord to touch your life—offer Him your hurt and your pain and trust in the power of His love.

Jesus Your Name

Jesus, Your name is power,

Jesus, Your name is might.

Jesus, Your name will break every stronghold.

Jesus, Your name is life.

Jesus, Your name is healing,

Jesus, Your name gives sight.

Jesus, Your name will free every captive,

Jesus, Your name is life.

Jesus, Your name is holy.

Jesus, Your name brings light.

Jesus, Your name is above every other.

Jesus, Your name is life.

—MORRIS CHAPMAN AND CLAIRE CLONINGER

*J*esus has many names. He called Himself the Son of Man, emphasizing His humanity (John 3:13). He called Himself the bread of life. Bread, giving sustenance and energy, refers to His role as a giver of life—eternal life (John 6:35). He referred to Himself as the gate for the sheep; He also called Himself the good shepherd (John 10:7, 11). Those names focused on His love and guidance, affirming that He is the only way to God's kingdom.

The most powerful of His names is "the resurrection and the life" (John 11:25), for this embodies all of the healing, power, light, might, and holiness that cause us to bow down in praise. Powerful things can happen when we call upon the name of Jesus—the disciples healed the sick in the name of Jesus, the dead were raised in the name of Jesus!

Think about the names you have for Jesus: Faithful Friend, Deliverer, Healer, Master, Savior, precious Lord, King of kings. Each name is an accurate description of Him. What is He to you today? Do you need power and might to face a battle ahead? Call on His name. Do you need to break strongholds in your life or experience healing? Call on His name. Call on the name of Jesus, for His name is above every other.

Therefore God exalted him to the highest place and gave him the name that is above every name, that at the name of Jesus every knee should bow, in heaven and on earth and under the earth.

PHILIPPIANS 2:9–10

PRAYER

Call Jesus by the name that means the most to you today. Thank Him that His name brings healing and life.

Times of Refreshing

Times of refreshing here in Your presence,

No greater blessing than being with You.

My soul is restored, my mind is renewed.

There's no greater joy, Lord,

Than being with You.

—DON HARRIS AND MARTY NYSTROM

*T*here is no greater joy than to be with the Lord. Have you found that to be true in your own life? Do you anxiously sit down to open your Bible? Do you hurry with other tasks in order to have time to talk with God?

That's what Jesus did. The Bible tells us of many times when Jesus went off alone to be with His Father. Mark wrote that "very early in the morning, while it was still dark, Jesus got up, left the house and went off to a solitary place, where he prayed" (Mark 1:35). The life of Christ is our example. If Jesus needed to meet with His heavenly Father, how much more do we! Only by communicating with Him will we learn to walk in His ways and be able to follow Him step by step. When we follow where He leads, He promises to make our paths straight (Proverbs 3:5–6). He longs for us to follow Him because He knows what good and wonderful things He has in store, just down the road.

Seek God in the morning and all day long. Experience His refreshment, enjoy His blessings. Let your soul be restored and your mind renewed. Experience the great joy of being with your Lord!

Repent, then, and turn to God, so that your sins may be wiped out, that times of refreshing may come from the Lord, and that he may send the Christ, who has been appointed for you—even Jesus.

ACTS 3:19–20

PRAYER

Find time alone to focus on God. Experience His refreshment. Ask Him to restore your soul and renew your mind. Enjoy Him!

I Need You More

I need You more, more than yesterday,

I need You, Lord, more than words can say.

I need You more than ever before,

I need You, Lord, I need You, Lord.

More than the air I breathe,

more than the song I sing,

More than the next heartbeat,

more than anything.

And Lord as time goes by,

I'll be by Your side

'Cause I never want to go back to my old life.

Right here in Your presence is where I belong,

This old broken heart has finally found a home

And I'll never be alone.

—LINDELL COOLEY AND BRUCE HAYNES

When we truly love someone, that love grows deeper day by day. We come to realize that we indeed love that person more than yesterday, and our love will continue to grow deeper on into the future.

The same holds true with our love for Jesus. As time goes by, the more we know Him, the more we love Him. We needed Him to cleanse us and make our lives whole, and He met that need! Now we find that we continue to need Him more and more every day because we are learning to trust Him more and more each day.

His grace is sufficient for us and His love is never-ending. What a blessing to know that the old life is gone for good. Because we have been freed from a life of brokenness and have entered the presence of the Lord, we will never be alone again.

More than a breath of fresh air, more than a heartbeat, we need the Lord. Without Him, life would be lonely, sad, and empty—and death would mean eternal separation from Him. We were meant to be filled with His Spirit. We belong in His presence.

Don't be ashamed to tell Jesus, "I need You more—more even than I needed You yesterday!" It's not a sign of weakness; it's a sign of coming home where you belong.

The LORD is good, a refuge in times of trouble. He cares for those who trust in him.

NAHUM 1:7

PRAYER

Tell the Lord how much you need Him. Praise Him for healing your broken heart and staying by your side.

I Need You / Strength of My Life

Lord, look upon my need, I need You,

I need You.

Oh Lord, have mercy now on me,

forgive me,

Oh Lord, forgive me and I will be clean.

Oh Lord, You are familiar with my ways,

There is nothing hid from You.

Oh Lord, You know the number of my days,

I want to live my life for You.

Every day I look to You to be the strength

of my life,

You're the hope I hold on to, be the strength

of my life.

—RICK FOUNDS / LESLIE PHILLIPS

*E*ven the strongest people will, at some point, need to slow down and rest. They have need of the power of Christ just as much as the weak.

Those who are strong often have difficulty admitting their need for mercy, for forgiveness. But Jesus didn't die just for those who are weak—He died for all of us! He knows everything about us from the way we go about our day to our deepest needs; He even knows the number of our days on this earth! He created us, He will sustain us, and He will always be there to help us when we call.

Unlike us, He will never grow tired or weary. He is the strength that keeps us going day after day. We all have twenty-four hours in a day, seven days in a week, and fifty-two weeks in a year—we must use the days given to us to honor Him.

No one can fathom His mercy and understanding or His willingness to meet all of our needs. When you feel the crushing weight of life on this earth, admit your need and call upon God to renew your strength. He will answer. "Be strong and take heart, all you who hope in the LORD" (Psalm 31:24).

The LORD is my strength and my shield; my heart trusts in him, and I am helped. My heart leaps for joy and I will give thanks to him in song.

PSALM 28:7

PRAYER

Praise Him for being the strength of your life, and for knowing everything about you and still loving and forgiving you.

I Want to Be More Like You

I want to be more like You,

I want to be more like You,

I want to be a vessel You work through,

I want to be more like You.

—CLINT BROWN

"*I* want to be more like You" is a prayer we should pray continuously. Paul told the Philippians, "Your attitude should be the same as that of Christ Jesus" (Philippians 2:5).

Being like Jesus is not an easy task. Jesus was a living sacrifice. In His humility, He was willing to give up His life in order to do the will of His Father and provide salvation for us all. For us to imitate that would require sacrificing our selfishness and pride; it would require dying to ourselves and accepting His lordship over us. The tough thing about a living sacrifice is, it wants to crawl off the altar and run away—it doesn't want to die!

So how can we be more like Jesus? Seems impossible. Fortunately, we don't have to do it on our own. The Holy Spirit within us teaches us humility and obedience. We can indeed be transformed; we can indeed be more like Him. The Bible says, "Those who become Christians become new persons. They are not the same anymore, for the old life is gone. A new life has begun!" (2 Corinthians 5:17 NLT).

Allow Jesus to change you, to transform your heart and mind, that you may be a vessel for His use. Cry out to Him today and every day, "Jesus, I want to be more like You!"

Dear friends, now we are children of God, and what we will be has not yet been made known. But we know that when he appears, we shall be like him, for we shall see him as he is.

1 JOHN 3:2

PRAYER

Repeat the words, "I want to be more like You," with sincerity and commitment. Pray that Jesus will help you be more like Him day by day.

God Is in the House

I've got Jesus, Jesus, He calls me for His own
And He lifts me, lifts me, above the world I know.
God is in the house, there is no doubt.
God is in the house, can't keep Him out.
As for you, as for me, we're gonna serve the Lord.

As for me, God came and found me,
As for me, He took me home,
As for me, He gave me a family
And I'll never walk alone.

In my life I'm soaked in blessing
And in Heav'n there's a great reward.
As for me and my house
We're gonna serve the Lord.

—RUSSELL FRAGAR AND DARLENE ZSCHECH

*I*s God at home in your home? In other words, does His presence permeate the atmosphere of your home? Does your family find a sanctuary of God's presence and peace when they walk through the front door? Do guests find a joyful welcome?

Too many homes are like war zones. There's anger, piercing words, painful hurts, even heavy silence. Even Christian homes are seldom sanctuaries of peace. We run from activity to activity, job to job, commitment to commitment. Lost is the art of conversation by a family around the dinner table. Seldom do guests come our way. Few and far between are the conversations with the neighbors next door or down the block.

God would not have it that way. He wants to lift us above the world we know and set us in a higher place. He wants us to look from His perspective. He would have us invite Him into our homes as a permanent Guest. He desires that our homes be little oases of peace, joy, and love in an all-too-often unpeaceful, joyless, unloving world.

What happens when you open your front door? Is God there? Begin today to make your home a place where God dwells, a place that invites your family and friends to come and experience Him.

And now, O Israel, what does the Lord your God ask of you but to fear the Lord your God, to walk in all his ways, to love him, to serve the Lord your God with all your heart and with all your soul.

DEUTERONOMY 10:12

PRAYER

Close your eyes and think about the atmosphere in your home. Ask God to dwell there constantly.

Above All Else

You are exalted Lord above all else,
We place You at the highest place
above all else.
Right now where we stand and
everywhere we go,
We place You at the highest place so the
world will know
You are a mighty warrior, dressed in
armor of light,
Crushing the deeds of darkness, lead us
on in the fight.
Through the blood of Jesus
Victorious we stand,
We place You at the highest place,
Above all else in this land.

—KIRK DEARMAN AND DEBY DEARMAN

Who is Jesus Christ to you? Is He just a prophet or great teacher, or is He the mighty warrior who has conquered the darkness of sin in your life?

As Christians, we know Jesus Christ is the Son of God sent down from heaven. Because of what He has done for us, we must place Him at the highest place in our lives—the throne of our hearts. Right now where we stand and everywhere we go, we must place Him front and center so that the world may know who He is and what He has done for us. When other people, even things, take priority in our lives, we must step back and take a look at what is most important. The psalmist said, "For you, O LORD, are the Most High over all the earth; you are exalted far above all gods" (Psalm 97:9). Therefore, the only place fit for Him is to be first and foremost in all we do.

Maybe you know *who* Jesus is to you, but *where* is He in your life? Have you put Him on the throne or locked Him in a closet? Today, talk to Him about placing Him in the highest place, central to all you do. When you do, you'll find victory—in this life and in the next.

The one who comes from above is above all; the one who is from the earth belongs to the earth, and speaks as one from the earth. The one who comes from heaven is above all.

JOHN 3:31

PRAYER

Ask the Lord to take the throne of your life that you may hold Him above all else.

DAY 37

O Most High

O Most High, You who are my stronghold,
When troubles come, You're my hiding place.
O Most High, those who know
You trust You,
You will not forsake the ones who
seek Your face.
I will give thanks to the Lord with
all my heart,
I will sing glorious praises to Your name.
I will be glad and exalting You, my Lord
Yesterday, today, forever, You're the same.

—CLAY HECOCKS

Change can be very threatening. We don't like to see changes in the world—war looming and terrorists lurking. We don't like to see our friends' marriages dissolve, or watch them self-destruct in other ways. We don't like the change in the job we so enjoyed by the arrival of a new boss. We don't like the change in our church when things don't go as planned. Changes for the worse can be extremely painful. How we long for a change for the better.

Thankfully, we have a stronghold in this changing world. Our Lord is unchanging. He is the same loving and just Lord who created the heavens and the earth. He will be the same God when we see Him face to face in glory. He is our stronghold when we are besieged by the enemy. He is our hiding place when we need a refuge. And He will never forsake us when we seek Him.

Give thanks to the Lord with all your heart! He never changes— what an amazing comfort for us! The God who kept His promises to Abraham, guided Moses, gave strength to Joshua, loved David, forgave Peter, and empowered Paul is the same God who is at work in your life today. He has no need to change because He is perfect. His love, His sacrifice, and His grace have paved the way for your salvation. He can take care of the sins of your yesterdays, the struggles of your todays, and the worries about your tomorrows. So move forward with confidence, for the Lord Most High goes with you!

Jesus Christ is the same yesterday and today and forever.

HEBREWS 13:8

PRAYER

Are you facing a difficult change today? Talk to the unchanging God about your frustrations and fears. Be thankful that you can always count on Him.

Lord Most High

From the ends of the earth, from the depths
of the sea,
From the heights of the heavens,
Your name we praise.
From the hearts of the weak, from the shouts
of the strong,
From the lips of all people,
This song we raise.
Throughout the endless ages, You will be
crowned with praises,
Lord Most High, exalted in every nation,
Sovereign of all creation,
Lord Most High, be magnified.

—DON HARRIS AND GARY SADLER

*S*tories of God's love and understanding are passed down from parent to child, from generation to generation. When we hear stories of God touching the lives of our parents and grandparents, our hearts are warmed and our spirit rejoices. If we are the ones to begin the song for future generations, then we have a story to tell and plenty of praising to do!

We praise our Lord Most High for all He has done in our lives. We praise Him for the promises of the future, when every nation will bow and acknowledge that He is the rightful King of all. We praise Him for the earth itself that knows its Creator and blazes with color and sound in an effort to praise the living God.

Do you want to pass your faith along to your children or others in your sphere of influence? Then join in the chorus of praise that is echoing across all of creation. There is no place on earth where you could go that God will not be with you. If you climb the highest mountain peak, praise Him from there. If you dive to the depths of the sea, praise Him from there. If you're feeling weak, praise Him even with what little strength you have. When you do, God will be glorified and you will be a living example of the power of your Lord Most High.

Let them know that you, whose name is the LORD—that you alone are the Most High over all the earth.

PSALM 83:18

PRAYER

Pray that God will make Himself known in your life that others may see your example and join the song of praise.

77

Be Magnified

I have made You too small in my eyes,
oh Lord forgive me,
And I have believed in a lie that You were
unable to help me.
But now, oh Lord, I see my wrong, heal my
heart and show Yourself strong
And in my eyes and with my song, oh Lord,
be magnified.
Be magnified oh Lord, You are highly exalted
And there is nothing You can't do.
Oh Lord, my eyes are on You, be magnified,
oh Lord, be magnified.
I have leaned on the wisdom of men,
oh Lord forgive me.
And I have responded to them, instead
of Your light and Your mercy.
But now, oh Lord, I see my wrong,
Heal my heart and show Yourself strong,
And in my eyes and with my song
Oh Lord be magnified, oh Lord be magnified.

—LYNN DESHAZO

*I*t's so easy for us to try to go it alone, isn't it? We forge ahead, working on sheer emotion or will. We dash headlong into a situation thinking we can handle it all on our own. This is a *little* problem; why bother God with it?

Or, on the flip side, we *don't* go it alone; we just run away. The problem seems as big as an enemy army and so we hide in the castle, pulling up the drawbridge behind us. This is a *big* problem, maybe even too big for God. Or because it's a problem of our own making, we think God doesn't care.

In both cases, we've developed an out-of-focus view of God. We think He's too big to deal with our little problems, or He's too small to deal with our big problems. When we see God as smaller and less powerful than He is, we miss out on the blessings of His strength to help us. When we set aside His promises to be with us through *everything* we face—small or big, our own fault or not—we miss out on experiencing His mercy and grace to help us in our time of need.

Is your God too small? Then He needs to be magnified. Ask God to fix your vision and bring His power into clear sight for whatever situation you face today.

Oh, magnify the LORD *with me, and let us exalt His name together.*

PSALM 34:3 (NKJV)

PRAYER

Seek the Lord's forgiveness for the times when you have lost faith. Ask Him to open your eyes to His strength and glory that He may be magnified through you.

Redeemer, Savior, Friend

I know You had me on Your mind when you
climbed up on that hill,
For You saw me with eternal eyes while I was yet in sin.
Redeemer, Savior, Friend.
Every stripe upon Your battered back,
every thorn that pierced Your brow,
Every nail drove deep through guiltless hands
said that Your love knows no end.
Redeemer, Savior, Friend.
Redeemer, redeem my heart again, Savior,
come and shelter me from sin.
You're familiar with my weakness, devoted to the end,
Redeemer, Savior, Friend.
So the grace You poured upon my life will
return to You in praise.
I'll gladly lay down all my crowns
For the name by which I'm saved.
Redeemer, Savior, Friend.

—DARRELL EVANS AND CHRIS SPRINGER

The hill was Golgotha, located on a roadway outside of Jerusalem. The stripes on His back came from a leather whip studded at the ends with pieces of bone—designed to rip and tear flesh. The thorns had made a "crown," fashioned of branches from a thornbush, then pressed down upon His head. The nails pounded into His hands and feet secured Him to the wooden cross, guaranteeing a slow and agonizing death.

Why?

Because with His "eternal eyes," God had designed a way to bring sinful humanity to Himself. The blood sacrifices of the Old Testament became one perfect sacrificial Lamb hung on a cross, killed to take away sin. And when it was over, death and sin had been forever defeated and access was provided for sinful humanity to the throne of God.

Jesus was devoted to the end. Every thorn that pierced His brow, every nail that went through His guiltless hands, told how His love has no end.

He did this just for you. When He went to the cross, you were on His mind. If you had been the only person on the planet, He'd have done the same. He is your Redeemer, your Savior, and your Friend. What can you do for such a Friend? Thank Him, praise Him, love Him, live for Him.

Greater love has no one than this, that he lay down his life for his friends.

JOHN 15:13

PRAYER

Dwell upon what Christ went through for you. Thank Him for His sacrifice and praise Him for giving you life eternal through His name.

Hallowed Be Thy Name

You are love, You are life, You are Lord over everything,
Alpha, Omega, Jehovah the King of kings.
Wonderful Way-Maker, worthy of my offering,
hallowed be Thy name.
You're the answer to all of my problems and
You solve them,
You supply all my needs and I call You Abba Father,
You're a mighty fortress in the time of tribulation
And I'm more than a conqueror in every situation.
You're the only God and there will never be another,
Ten thousand angels couldn't say how much I love You.
So I'm gonna lift You up, Lord, higher and higher,
And all the world will see how You set my soul on fire,
Hallowed be Thy name.

—BABBIE MASON AND ROBERT LAWSON

allowed means holy, sacred. Above all that Jesus is to us, He is holy. He is set apart, perfect, untouched by sin, clean, pure. It was that very holiness that allowed Him to be the perfect sacrifice for our sins. Perfect God, perfect man, united to take the punishment for sin that we deserved. And because He is holy—hallowed—He is the only one worthy of our praise.

The song goes on to give us more names of Jesus, all found in the Bible. He is love (1 John 4:8), He is life (John 1:4), He is Lord over everything (Deuteronomy 10:17). He's the Alpha and Omega (Revelation 1:8) and the King of kings (1 Timothy 6:15). He makes a way for us (Isaiah 43:19).

We can go to Him with our problems and He will help us solve them (Psalm 34:19). In His grace and goodness, He will supply all our needs (Philippians 4:19). When difficult times threaten to close in upon us, He is a fortress into which we can run (Psalm 18:2); because He loves us, we are more than conquerors in all situations (Romans 8:37).

He is God—the one and only holy Lord, and He alone is worthy of your praise. The Bible overflows with His promises to you. Do you want your soul set on fire for God? Then meditate on all He has done for you, praise Him for His promises, and honor His holy name.

In this manner, therefore, pray: Our Father in heaven, hallowed be Your name.

MATTHEW 6:9 (NKJV)

PRAYER

Think about the holiness of Jesus, about how His name is sacred above all other names. Pray to Him with that in mind—that you are approaching the holy God who is worthy of your praise.

Jesus Is Mine

Jesus is mine, Jesus is mine,
Everywhere I go, everywhere I'll be,
Oh, Jesus is mine.
Mine in the morning, mine in the evening,
All the day long, singin' my song,
He's mine, oh yes, He's mine.

—AUTHOR UNKNOWN

*T*his is at once both a comforting and a convicting thought. How wonderful to know that Jesus is ours! He is with us wherever we go. In the morning and in the evening, all day long, with us wherever we go . . .

So where did your feet take you today? Were you aware of Jesus' presence? Did your knowledge of His proximity make a difference in what you said and how you acted? Do you think the people with whom you interacted might have been surprised to know that you claim the name of Jesus?

King David asked, "Where can I go from your Spirit? . . . If I go up to the heavens, you are there; if I make my bed in the depths, you are there. . . . If I settle on the far side of the sea, even there your hand will guide me" (Psalm 139:7–10). The apostle Paul exulted that nothing "in all creation, will be able to separate us from the love of God" (Romans 8:39). If Jesus is yours—your Savior and your Lord—rejoice in the fact of His presence!

But realize that this is also an awesome responsibility. You represent Christ wherever you go. By your actions and attitudes, you either draw people one step closer to Christ or you turn them off to Him. Everywhere you go, Jesus goes with you. Morning, evening, all day long!

Praise the LORD. Praise the LORD, O my soul. I will praise the LORD all my life; I will sing praise to my God as long as I live.

PSALM 146:1–2

PRAYER

Praise the Lord for His constant presence in your life—for being with you through every day of your life, and for all of eternity.

How Great Are You Lord

How great are You Lord,
how great is Your mercy,
How great are the things that
You have done for me.
How great are You, Lord,
Your loving kindness
Is filling my heart as I sing.
How great are You, Lord,
how great is Your love,
It reaches to the heavens.
How great is the heart
That sought and rescued me.

—LYNN DeSHAZO

*H*ow great are You, Lord! Considering all that God has done for us, an outburst of praise is only natural. We have so much to praise Him for!

Think of His mercy, His undeserved favor. We did nothing to cause Him to love us. We did not deserve His love, but He loved us anyway. Mercy alone caused Him to reach out to a dying world and give His life so that we might live.

Think of all that He has done for us. He redeemed us, saved us, called us to be His own, and sent us His Spirit to strengthen and guide us all the days of our lives.

Think of His kindness, that He lovingly reaches down to protect us when we are in danger, encourage us when we are downtrodden, comfort us when we are hurting.

Think of such love that would seek us and rescue us. Such love is unfathomable, such love is unimaginable, such love is drenched upon us from our great Lord.

Great is the LORD and most worthy of praise; his greatness no one can fathom.

PSALM 145:3

PRAYER

Remember that Jesus sought you in your sin and rescued you from it. Thank Him and praise Him for His greatness in your life.

Lead Me, O Lead Me

O lead me to the place where I can find You,

O lead me to the place where You'll be,

Lead me to the cross where we first met,

Draw me to my knees so we can talk,

Let me feel Your breath,

Let me know You're here with me.

—MARTIN SMITH

*M*ost of us are not content to follow—we like to lead! As human beings, we automatically want to go our own way, sure of ourselves that our way is the right way.

When we put aside our selfishness and pride, we can then admit that we don't know the way. We can acknowledge that we need to follow someone greater than ourselves—that we need to be led in the right direction.

God knows the direction our lives will take long before we are even capable of choosing what crayon to use in a coloring book. When we are willing to be led by the Spirit, He will bring us to Himself. He will show us the path of the cross and bring us to our knees. When we pour out our heart and soul to Him, He will listen. He is always present, always listening for our call, always waiting for us to ask for His leading in our lives.

What questions do you have today? What guidance do you need? Ask Jesus to meet you at the cross. Why there? Because when you look upon the cross, you cannot help but set aside all your pride, get down on your knees, and feel the very breath of God.

I will lead the blind by ways they have not known, along unfamiliar paths I will guide them; I will turn the darkness into light before them and make the rough places smooth. These are the things I will do; I will not forsake them.

ISAIAH 42:16

PRAYER

Pour out your heart to God and ask for His leading in every situation in your life.

Ah, Lord God

Ah, Lord God, Thou has made the heavens
And the earth by Thy great power.
Ah, Lord God, Thou has made the heavens
And the earth by Thine outstretched arm.
Nothing is too difficult for Thee,
Great and mighty God,
Great in counsel and mighty in deed,
Nothing, nothing, absolutely nothing,
Nothing is too difficult for Thee.

—KAY CHANCE

He desperately wanted a child, but both he and his wife were old. God had made a promise, but He certainly seemed to be in no hurry to keep it. Didn't God understand that there would be a certain age beyond which childbearing would be impossible?

Then God came once again, repeating the promise and asking, "Is anything too hard for the LORD?" (Genesis 18:14).

The prophet Jeremiah had warned the nation of Judah that God would punish them. Yet God had also promised to return His people to their land. To prove the reliability of that promise, God told His prophet to buy a plot of land—now in enemy hands. Not seemingly a very good investment.

Yet Jeremiah trusted God. "Nothing is too hard for you," he said (Jeremiah 32:17).

Fast-forward. Jesus has explained that it is difficult for the rich to enter the kingdom. The astonished disciples ask, "Who then can be saved?" (Matthew 19:25).

Jesus answered, "With man this is impossible, but with God all things are possible" (Matthew 19:26).

Our God is the God of the impossible. When the situation looks bleak, when all hope is gone, "with God all things are possible." When the problem is too big, ask yourself, "Is anything too hard for the Lord?" And then answer yourself, "Nothing is too difficult for Him!"

Ah Lord GOD! Behold, Thou hast made the heavens and the earth by Thy great power and by Thine outstretched arm! Nothing is too difficult for Thee.

JEREMIAH 32:17 (NASB)

PRAYER

Come to God with the knowledge that nothing is too difficult for Him—His counsel is perfect and His power is overwhelming.

D A Y 4 6

Jesus, We Celebrate Your Victory

Jesus, we celebrate Your victory, Jesus,
we revel in Your love,
Jesus, we rejoice, You've set us free, Jesus,
Your death has brought us life.
It was for freedom that Christ has set us free,
No longer to be subject to a yoke of slavery.
So we're rejoicing in God's victory,
our hearts responding to His love.
His Spirit in us releases us from fear
And the way to Him is open, with
boldness we draw near.
And in His presence our problems disappear,
Our hearts responding to His love.

—JOHN GIBSON

*W*e celebrate His victory because His victory means we also have victory! Satan had his major victories in the Garden of Eden and at the Cross (or so he thought). But God turned Satan's victory into utter and devastating defeat when Jesus rose from the dead.

Death no longer brings fear to our hearts. "Where, O death, is your victory? Where, O death, is your sting?" (1 Corinthians 15:55). Jesus defeated death when He broke through its grasp and rose from the grave. We now have hope that extends beyond the grave and into eternity!

Jesus has set us free from the bondage of sin, from the stronghold of death, and from the power of Satan. His Spirit releases us from fear. Jesus opened the door from death to life and gave us the victory.

With the door now open, we can enter the presence of the Lord. We can draw near to Him and respond to His love. He will flood our hearts with peace and our problems will disappear in the presence of His greatness. "For everyone born of God overcomes the world. This is the victory that has overcome the world, even our faith" (1 John 5:4).

We can celebrate our victory in Jesus, because He is victorious over all!

Death has been swallowed up in victory.

1 CORINTHIANS 15:54

PRAYER

Thank the Lord for His victory over sin and death, and for passing on that victory to you.

This Kingdom

Jesus, God's righteousness revealed, the Son of Man,
the Son of God,
His Kingdom come, Jesus redemption's sacrifice
Now glorified, now justified, His Kingdom come.
And this Kingdom will know no end, and its glory
shall know no bounds,
For the majesty and power of this Kingdom's
King has come
And this Kingdom's reign, and this Kingdom's rule,
And this Kingdom's power and authority,
Jesus, God's righteousness revealed.
Jesus, the expression of God's love, the grace of God,
The Word of God revealed to us.
Jesus, God's holiness displayed, now glorified,
now justified,
His Kingdom come.

—GEOFF BULLOCK

*T*he Pharisees asked Jesus when the kingdom of God would come. They were looking for a kingdom on earth in which God would vanquish all enemies and become a ruler. Jesus responded to their question by telling them that the kingdom of God "is within you" (Luke 17:20–21). The kingdom of God is the work of the Holy Spirit within the hearts of those who trust in Jesus.

The kingdom of God is here—it is now. If we have given our hearts to Jesus, if we have committed ourselves to His power, His kingdom is within us! The grace of God, His word, and His holiness are displayed for all to see as His will is done in us and as we live to honor Him.

But make no mistake. There will indeed be a physical kingdom—a time when Christ shall reign on this earth. We *are* awaiting that kingdom, anticipating its arrival with joy. In that kingdom, "the dwelling of God is with men, and he will live with them. . . . He will wipe every tear from their eyes. There will be no more death or mourning or crying or pain, for the old order of things has passed away" (Revelation 21:3–4).

This kingdom will know no end. Its glory will know no bounds. This kingdom is ours because of Christ Jesus. "Amen. Come Lord Jesus."

Your kingdom is an everlasting kingdom, and your dominion endures through all generations. The LORD is faithful to all his promises and loving toward all he has made.

PSALM 145:13

PRAYER

Pray the Lord's Prayer, knowing that His kingdom has come in your heart because you have placed your faith in Him.

The Happy Song

Oh I could sing unending songs of how
You saved my soul.
Well I could dance a thousand miles
because of Your great love.
My heart is bursting, Lord, to tell of
all You've done,
Of how You've changed my life and
wiped away the past.
I wanna shout it out, from every rooftop sing
For now I know that God is for me, not against me.
Everybody's singing now 'cause we're so happy.
Everybody's dancing now 'cause we're so happy.
If only we could see His face and
see Him smiling over us
And unseen angels celebrate for joy is in this place.

—MARTIN SMITH

*N*ehemiah's task had not been easy. Called by God to return to Jerusalem and encourage the rebuilding of the city's wall, Nehemiah had faced numerous setbacks and frustrations—enough to make most of us mount our donkeys and be gone. But not Nehemiah. No matter what new opposition surfaced, Nehemiah constantly prayed for God's guidance and encouraged the people. Under his leadership, the people finished the wall in fifty-two days.

The next step was to remind the people of the law of God. When Ezra read the law, the people realized how far they had strayed, and they wept. But Nehemiah told them to focus on the future, to commit to serving God. "This day is sacred to our Lord. Do not grieve, for the joy of the LORD is your strength" (Nehemiah 8:10).

Perhaps you feel convicted by God's Word. Sin seems to overwhelm you. Take courage from Nehemiah's example. Begin rebuilding your relationship with God. Mourn for your past sins, but then commit to obedience in the future. Let this be a day of rejoicing. Let your voice sing and your feet dance! Tell others how He saved you and how He changed your life.

Shout it out—sing from the rooftops! Let your joy be heard far beyond the confines of your heart. Everybody sing, everybody dance—joy is in this place!

And on that day they offered great sacrifices, rejoicing because God had given them great joy. The women and children also rejoiced. The sound of rejoicing in Jerusalem could be heard far away.

NEHEMIAH 12:43

PRAYER

Rejoice that the Lord has wiped away the past and saved your soul. Praise Him with all of your being.

Days of Elijah

These are the days of Elijah, declaring the Word
of the Lord,
And these are the days of Your servant Moses,
Righteousness being restored.
And though these are days of great trials,
Of famine and darkness and sword,
Still we are the voice in the desert crying,
"Prepare ye the way of the Lord."
Behold He comes riding on the clouds,
Shining like the sun at the trumpet call,
Lift your voice, it's the year of Jubilee,
Out of Zion's hill salvation comes.
And these are the days of Ezekiel,
The dry bones becoming as flesh,
And these are the days of Your servant David,
Rebuilding a temple of praise.
And these are the days of the harvest,
The fields are as white in Your world.
And we are the laborers in Your vineyard,
Declaring the Word of the Lord.

—ROBIN MARK

In the Old Testament, the year of Jubilee was meant to be celebrated every fifty years. This would have been a time of great rejoicing among the Israelites. As dictated in Leviticus 25, all debts were to be cancelled, all land returned to its original owners, and all slaves set free.

Unfortunately, there is no record of this celebration ever being carried out. But when Jesus came, He gave every one of us a year of Jubilee, not just once every fifty years, but every day! Thanks to His sacrifice, our debts of sin are cancelled whenever we ask, we are promised a place in eternity, and we are made free by the power of His love.

Such good news must be shared! We may feel like voices in the desert, but we need to call out this wonderful message to all who will hear, just as the prophets Elijah, Moses, and Ezekiel did so many years ago.

The fields are ready to be harvested. Will you join the prophets of old in sharing the message of forgiveness, freedom, and a fantastic future?

Oh, that salvation for Israel would come out of Zion! . . . Look, he is coming with the clouds, and every eye will see him.

PSALM 53:6; REVELATION 1:7

PRAYER

Ask the Lord to help you share the joy of your salvation so others may know the freedom of jubilee.

I See the Lord

I see the Lord, I see the Lord,
Exalted high upon the worship of the people
of the earth.
I see the Lord, I see the Lord,
My eyes have seen the King, the Lamb
upon the throne
Who reigns forevermore.
The train of His robe fills the temple,
A cloud of heavenly worship surrounding
His throne.
We join with them now crying,
Holy, holy is the Lamb, the Lamb alone.
Forever and ever, forever and ever
Forevermore.

—JOHN CHISUM AND DON MOEN

*I*n our daily lives, filled with pressure and frustration, we often don't see God as He really is. We tend to push Him aside, too busy to focus on His holiness.

This song gives us a sense of the greatness of the Lord. When we recognize how great God is, we realize how we could never enter His presence if not for what Jesus did for us. We who were unclean and impure have received forgiveness. We have been given the ability to see the Lord in all of His holiness and power. We have been given the honor of being called heirs of the King, able to be in His presence forever and evermore.

The Lord, the Lamb upon the throne, is surrounded by praise. The Book of Revelation gives us a snapshot: "Each of the four living creatures had six wings and was covered with eyes all around, even under his wings. Day and night they never stop saying: 'Holy, holy, holy is the Lord God Almighty, who was, and is, and is to come'" (Revelation 4:8).

We can cry out in fellowship with all believers that Jesus Christ is holy—He is the Lamb and He alone is worthy of our praise. So join with the heavenly worshipers and proclaim the holiness and glory of the Lord!

They will see his face, and his name will be on their foreheads. There will be no more night. They will not need the light of a lamp or the light of the sun, for the Lord God will give them light. And they will reign for ever and ever.

REVELATION 22:4–5

PRAYER

Ask the Lord to help you to see Him high and exalted. Praise Him for His power and glory.

Sing, Shout, Clap

Sing, shout, clap your hands,

Give praise unto your Maker.

Make a joyful noise unto the Lord,

Sing, shout, clap your hands,

Give praise unto your Maker.

For the Lord, He is Almighty God.

This is the day of celebration,

This is the day to rejoice, rejoice.

The Lord our God is our deliverer,

So let's just praise His name.

—BILLY FUNK

The Book of Psalms is a collection of songs and prayers to the Lord. The writers chose to sing their praises to God and record their songs so that others, ourselves included, would someday join them in praise. The words they sang are timeless, applying to our lives even today.

Just as in days long past, we who believe in God demonstrate our joy when we sing, shout, and clap our hands. We can make a joyful noise unto the Lord!

Our reasons for praise are many, and the depth of our gratitude may sometimes leave us speechless. But when we sing songs exalting His holiness, shout for the joy of our salvation, and clap our hands in gratitude for all He has done for us, He responds with unmeasured blessings.

The songs we sing give praise to our Maker. The shout of the righteous has the power to tear down walls. Our hands rejoice that the Lord our God is our Deliverer. So, sing, shout, and clap your hands for this is the day to rejoice!

Come, let us sing for joy to the LORD; let us shout aloud to the Rock of our salvation.

PSALM 95:1

PRAYER

Sing for joy to the Lord; shout aloud to the Rock of your salvation; clap your hands in gratitude for all He has done for you.

You Are Crowned with Many Crowns

You are crowned with many crowns
And rule all things in righteousness.
You are crowned with many crowns
Upholding all things by Your Word.
You rule in power and reign in glory,
You are Lord of Heaven and earth.
You are Lord of all,
You are Lord of all.

—JOHN SELLERS

*J*esus first came to earth as a helpless baby. He was born of the Virgin Mary, grew up learning the family business (carpentry), and didn't begin His ministry until He was thirty years old. As a human being, He suffered at the hands of other human beings. He became like a Lamb, sacrificed for the sins of everyone. He came first to redeem us.

When Jesus comes again, He will come as the ultimate conqueror and King of all kings. He will wear the crowns of all nations. He will rule with power. He will bring judgment to the people of the earth. He will rule in power and reign in glory. He will separate those who know and obey Him from those who do not (2 Thessalonians 1:7–10). Those who have accepted His forgiveness will stand before Him without fear for He will claim them as His own children. Those who have rejected Him will, in turn, be rejected.

Which group will you be in? If you know Him and love Him, you will join with the multitude, rejoicing and giving Him the glory. He *is* returning, He *is* Lord of heaven and earth. Your acceptance or denial of these facts does not change them, but it does change *you*—both for now and for eternity.

His eyes are like blazing fire, and on his head are many crowns. He has a name written on him that no one knows but he himself.

REVELATION 19:12

PRAYER

If you have accepted Christ as your Lord, rejoice that you will someday stand before God and be recognized as His child. If not, what is keeping you from taking that step?

In Him We Live

In Him we live and move
And have our being.
Make a joyful noise,
Sing unto the Lord,
Tell Him of your love,
Dance before Him.
Make a joyful noise,
Sing unto the Lord,
Tell Him of your love.
Hallelujah.

—RANDY SPEIR

*W*hen we awake each morning, some of us hop out of bed and greet the day with a smile; some of us hit the snooze button and groan as we pull the covers over our head. Eventually, we face the day—we "live and move and have our being."

No matter how we greet the dawn, we should be thankful for each day we are given. Whether you've jumped out of bed in joyous anticipation or are still hiding under the covers, you can take a few moments to pray—asking God's guidance for every step of your day. In Him you live and move and have your being—so ask Him to make you a good example for Him throughout your day, at work, at school, in the store, on the road. Ask Him to keep you keenly aware of His presence to guide, help, and comfort each step of the way.

Then get out of bed and, if you can do it, sing unto the Lord! If you can't sing that early, then just tell Him of your love—He is the reason you live. Need some early morning exercise? Dance before Him—He is the reason you move. If your voice leaves something to be desired, then just make a joyful noise—He is the reason you have your being!

"For in him we live and move and have our being." As some of your own poets have said, "We are his offspring."

ACTS 17:28

PRAYER

Thank the Lord for giving you a reason to live. Ask Him to teach you what it means to live, move, and have your being in Him.

I Love to Praise Him

I love to praise Him,
I love to praise Him
And lift up His holy name.
Singing hallelujah,
Singing hallelujah,
Singing hallelujah
Unto Jesus my Lord,
We exalt Him on high.

—JENNIFER RANDOLPH

*T*he Bible is full of people praising God! They loved to praise Him then just as we love to praise Him today—and probably for many of the same reasons. Here are some examples:

"You will have plenty to eat, until you are full, and you will praise the name of the LORD your God, who has worked wonders for you" (Joel 2:26).

"Seven times a day I praise you for your righteous laws" (Psalm 119:164).

"I thank and praise you, O God of my fathers: You have given me wisdom and power" (Daniel 2:23).

"He jumped to his feet and began to walk. Then he went with them into the temple courts, walking and jumping, and praising God" (Acts 3:8).

"Jehoshaphat appointed men to sing to the LORD and to praise him for the splendor of his holiness as they went out at the head of the army, saying: 'Give thanks to the LORD, for his love endures forever'" (2 Chronicles 20:21).

Now, just as in biblical times, we praise God for providing our basic needs, for teaching us rules to live by, for giving us wisdom and power, for healing our brokenness, and most importantly, for His holiness and His love which endure forever.

Sing hallelujah and lift up His holy name. Praise and exalt the Lord on high for He has done great things!

But you are a chosen people, a royal priesthood, a holy nation, a people belonging to God, that you may declare the praises of him who called you out of darkness into his wonderful light.

1 PETER 2:9

PRAYER

What can you praise God for today? For meeting your needs? For providing you with His Word? For giving you wisdom and power to handle a certain situation? For healing and help? For His holiness and love? Be specific as you praise Him.

Change My Heart Oh God

Change my heart, O God
Fill me with Your Spirit,
Take away desires that drive me far from You.
Whisper from Your Word, help my heart to hear it.
Fill me with desire to follow You.
No matter where You lead me,
No matter how I'm tested,
I believe You can help me grow
And help me to obey.

—ED KERR

A true desire to change comes from a heart that trusts in Jesus. Before we put our faith in Him, we could not understand spiritual things. We couldn't comprehend God or how He could possibly work in our lives.

While no one, believer or non-believer, can ever fully comprehend God, by the help of His Spirit we can be led to obey and grow. The Spirit will whisper in our hearts and fill us with the desire to follow the Lord.

In 1 Corinthians 2:14, the apostle Paul tells us that those without the Spirit of God cannot understand or accept the things that come from the Spirit. Why? Because the lines of communication were never established. Because they were not willing to change, to grow, or to obey the Spirit of the Lord.

Praise the Lord that He provided His Spirit to those who trust in Him. He has taken away the desires that drive us from Him and has replaced them with the desire to follow Christ. No matter where He leads, we will follow. We will trust and obey.

We have not received the spirit of the world but the Spirit who is from God, that we may understand what God has freely given us.

1 CORINTHIANS 2:12

PRAYER

Make the words of this song your prayer. Ask God to change your heart, take away desires that drive you from Him, and fill you with a desire to follow and obey.

Blessed Be the Name of the Lord

Blessed be the name of the Lord,
Life and power to all it brings,
Peace and healing within His wings.
He's the Lord of Glory, the King of kings.
His name is Eternal Father, His name is
the Bread of Life,
His name overcomes the darkness,
His name is a great light.
His name is a wall of fire, no evil can penetrate,
His name is the Lord Almighty,
His name is a shield of faith.
Call upon Him, enter His courts with praise,
Call upon Him, seek His face.
His name is Yahweh, Redeemer,
Messiah, Jehovah, Prince of Peace, Deliverer,
The Soon and Coming King,
Almighty God, blessed be His name forever.

—MARK LEVANG AND CATHY RISO

*B*lessed be the name of the Lord, for that name brings life and power to all who call. His name is many different things to many people, and each name describes His attributes.

He is the Lord of Glory, Lord Almighty, and the King of kings—strength, power, and majesty pour down from His throne. He is the Eternal Father—we can run to Him with our problems and He will lovingly guide us. He is the Bread of Life—He sustains us and provides for our most basic human needs. He is Yahweh, Redeemer, Deliverer—He purchased our freedom with His own blood as the payment for our sins. He is Messiah, Jehovah—the Anointed One who delivers us. He is the Prince of Peace—no one else could bring peace to our hearts, minds, and souls. He is the Soon and Coming King—those who know Him will meet Him in the air.

Every aspect of our lives is enveloped by the many names of the Lord. He brings light to the darkness and healing to the broken spirit. When we seek Him in all of His righteousness and glory, we find exactly what we need, for He is everything to everyone in every situation. All we need to do is call on Him. Blessed be the name of the Lord!

And everyone who calls on the name of the Lord will be saved.

ACTS 2:21

PRAYER

Call upon the name of the Lord and He will answer. Call upon Him with the name that most matches your need today—Father, Bread of Life, Redeemer, Deliverer.

No Higher Calling

Down at Your feet, O Lord
Is the most high place.
In Your presence, Lord,
I seek Your face.
I seek Your face.
There is no higher calling
No greater honor than to bow
And kneel before Your throne.
I'm amazed at Your glory,
Embraced by Your mercy,
O Lord, I live to worship You.

—GREG GULLEY AND LENNY LEBLANC

*K*neeling humbly at the feet of Jesus is the highest place we could be. Two women who were contemporaries of Jesus found this out for themselves.

Mary, the sister of Lazarus and Martha, welcomed Jesus into her home. While her sister was preparing the meal, Mary chose to sit at the feet of Jesus listening to what He said. Jesus praised her, saying she had chosen what was better—spending time with Him. Her devotion was more important than anything else (Luke 10:38–42).

At another time, Mary again sat at Jesus' feet, this time pouring expensive perfume on Jesus' feet and wiping them with her hair. Her sacrifice provided a lesson for the disciples about the divinity of Jesus (John 12:1–11).

In a separate, yet similar incident, a woman referred to only as having "lived a sinful life" entered the house where Jesus was a guest and knelt at His feet. She, too, poured perfume on His feet and it mingled with her tears. Jesus extended the ultimate gift to her for her love and devotion when He said to her, "Your sins are forgiven" (Luke 7:38–50). She was embraced by His mercy.

We, too, will find our highest glory and our highest calling when we humbly kneel at His feet.

*Come, let us bow down in worship, let us kneel before the L*ORD *our Maker.*

PSALM 95:6

PRAYER

Kneel as you come into the presence of the Lord. Pray that He will embrace you with His power, His glory, and His mercy.

More of You

All I want is more of You,
All I want is more of You,
Nothing I desire, Lord,
But more of You, more of You.
Jesus, I am thirsty,
Won't You come and fill me?
Earthly things have left me dry,
Only You can satisfy,
All I want is more of You.

—DON HARRIS AND MARTIN J. NYSTROM

When we come to the end of a long and tiring day, when our strength and energy are depleted, we need something to revive us. As a long, cool drink of water quenches our thirst on a sizzling day, so we need something to quench our thirst for meaning behind all of the endless activity of life. The world offers only empty platitudes, leaving us dry and unfulfilled.

When we let Jesus quench our thirst, however, we find that He fills us up to overflowing. As the psalmist said, "My cup overflows" (Psalm 23:5). And He fills us with living water. As He told the woman at the well, "The water I give them takes away thirst altogether. It becomes a perpetual spring within them, giving them eternal life" (John 4:14 NLT).

So Jesus says to you, "If you are thirsty, come to me!" (John 7:37 NLT). When you thirst for meaning, purpose, revival, or restoration, you need only to seek the Lord and ask for more of the living water. All you could ever need or desire can be found in Him, and He is faithful to satisfy.

All you want is more—that's not asking much when you know that the source is unending, that the river will never run dry. Say to Him, "All I want is more of You!"

If you are thirsty, come to me! If you believe in me, come and drink! For the Scriptures declare that rivers of living water will flow out from within.

JOHN 7:37–38 (NLT)

PRAYER

Ask the Lord for more—more of His mercy, His love, and His presence in your life. Ask Him to fill you to overflowing that you may be an example of His love.

Prepare the Way

He has come to bring light into the darkness,

He has come to bring freedom to the captives,

He has come to restore the brokenhearted,

It's time to proclaim the year of the Lord.

Prepare the way, prepare the way

for our Redeemer,

Prepare the way, prepare the way

for our Restorer.

Make ready your heart, make ready your home,

Make ready the people of God.

Prepare the way.

He has come to bring hope to the hopeless,

He has come to comfort all who mourn,

He has come to heal our every sickness.

It's time to proclaim the year of the Lord.

Prepare the way of the Lord.

—DARRELL EVANS AND ERIC NUZUM

*I*f you're like most people, the occasion of guests coming to your home requires preparation, perhaps scooping up piles of stuff and tossing it into the back reaches of your house, carefully closing the door on the mess. A quick swipe at piles of dust makes your home presentable. Why do we go through this? Because we want to present our best selves.

Jesus is coming—He announced it long ago. The only problem is that He didn't say *when* He would arrive. To make our hearts and our homes ready for Jesus requires something more than stashing extraneous material behind closed doors, however. It means we need to keep our lives free of the clutter of useless thoughts or harmful activities. It means not allowing the dust to collect on our obedience and faithfulness. It means we are constantly watching, always ready for His arrival.

John the Baptist prepared the people to meet Jesus. They came to him confessing their sins. As Christians today preparing the way for Jesus, we should follow the example of those early converts. The apostle Paul later wrote, "So be careful how you live, not as fools but as those who are wise. Make the most of every opportunity for doing good in these evil days" (Ephesians 5:15–16 NLT).

Is your heart ready for Jesus' return? Is your life helping to prepare the way for others to meet Him as well?

It is written in Isaiah the prophet: "I will send my messenger ahead of you, who will prepare your way"—"a voice of one calling in the desert, 'Prepare the way for the Lord, make straight paths for him.'"

M A R K   1 : 2 – 3

P R A Y E R

Ask the Lord to show you where you might need to do some cleanup work in your heart. Ask Him to help you prepare others for Him to make His way into their hearts and lives.

New Song Arisin'

There's a new song arisin' in the hearts
of His children,
A new song arisin' in the hearts of His own,
A song of hope, a song of peace,
The sound of liberation,
The shout of victory.
The hymn of praise, the new song of God,
Many will see and fear and put their
trust in our Lord.
With the oil of joy, He's anointing His children,
The music He gives sets the nations free,
And the dance of our Father's bringing liberty.

—DARRELL EVANS

*S*ometimes we wonder if God hears our prayers. We pray and plead, and then we wait. Sometimes, the waiting is the hardest part. But we can rest assured that God *does* hear us when we call—He *will* answer our prayers and give us a new song, a hymn of praise to sing of our joy!

Take Abraham for example. He prayed and asked God for a son; *twenty-four years later*, God granted his request and Isaac was born. "Is anything too hard for the LORD?" the angels asked Abraham in Genesis 18:14. In the heart of Abraham was a song of hope, a song of peace—God had blessed him with a child.

We can have that same joy when we put our trust in the Lord! We can sing a new song, one of hope and peace, liberation and victory. "The music He gives sets the nations free." As His children, we know He hears our prayers as well as our praises. His song sets us free!

What are the needs in your life? Take them to the Lord in prayer and trust that He will answer. Put your hope in the One who gives you a new song to sing, for the music He gives is unlike any other in the world. Sing with a joyful heart! Hallelujah!

He put a new song in my mouth, a hymn of praise to our God. Many will see and fear and put their trust in the LORD.

PSALM 40:3

PRAYER

Ask the Lord for peace in all aspects of your life. Tell Him your needs and your hopes and ask Him to put a new song in your heart as you put your trust in Him.

D A Y   6 1

Stand Up and Give Him the Praise

Who is like the Lord? There is no one.
Who is like the Lord? He is strong and mighty.
Who is like the Lord? He is worthy.
Stand up and give Him the praise.
Praise the Lord, praise the Lord, our God is
worthy of glory.
From the rising of the sun to its going down,
The name of the Lord is to be praised.
Stand up and praise Him and give Him the glory,
Stand up and praise Him and give Him the glory,
Our God is worthy of praise.

—LYNN DeSHAZO

*M*any have attempted to set themselves up as "gods." Confucius and Buddha were men of great wisdom. Hare Krishna spoke of peace. The Dalai Lama tells others how to show kindness and compassion. Movements, cults, and full-fledged religions surround these men, but they all have one thing in common—they were and are just human beings. Confucius, Buddha, and Krishna are dead and they never rose from the grave. Someday, the Dalai Lama will meet the same fate.

Like those self-made gods, Jesus spoke of peace and love and showed compassion to those who needed it the most. Unlike them, however, He was capable of more: He healed the sick and even raised the dead. He walked on water and calmed the raging storm. He offered Himself to God as a payment for our sins that we might not face the judgment of God. And He did something else that no one else has done—He rose from the dead and ascended into heaven, never to die again! Now, He sits at the right hand of God interceding for us and forgiving our sins.

So stand up and give Him the praise! The Lord strong and mighty, He is the only one worthy. There never was and never shall be anyone like Him. No one in heaven, on earth, or under the earth is like our Lord and Savior, Jesus Christ.

Who among the gods is like you, O LORD? Who is like you—majestic in holiness, awesome in glory, working wonders?

EXODUS 15:11

PRAYER

Praise Him for being the one and only true God, working wonders in your life and forgiving your sins. Give Him the glory He deserves.

Breathe on Me

Breathe on me breath of God,

Love and life that makes me free.

Breathe on me breath of God,

Fan the flame within me.

Teach my heart, heal my soul,

Speak the mind that in Christ we know.

Take me to Your sanctuary, breathe on me.

Speak to me voice of God,

Soft and still inside my heart,

Speak to me Word of God,

Comfort, heal, restore, with love.

Breathe on me.

—LUCY FISHER

*O*ur God is all-powerful. When He wants our attention, He will get it! Sometimes He does it in unexpected ways.

Elijah was frightened. He'd experienced great victory against the prophets of Baal—proving that God alone was to be worshiped. But that hadn't stopped the contract put out on his life by wicked Queen Jezebel. Elijah ran away, afraid for his life and certain that he was the only one left who truly believed in God.

When God wanted to speak to His discouraged servant Elijah, He took him up on the mountain and told him that He Himself would pass by. Then came a wind powerful enough to shatter rocks, an earthquake, and a fire—but the Lord was not in any of those things. Instead, His voice came to Elijah in a quiet whisper (1 Kings 19:9–13).

When Elijah heard the voice, he went out and talked to God. Elijah told the Lord his fears and worries. The quiet and soothing voice of God responded with comfort and with a further assignment, getting Elijah back on track.

When you are weighed down by fear, doubt, and worry, you may need to sit quietly and simply ask God to breathe on you. He will restore your weary soul and speak to your heart with His gentle whisper.

Can you hear it?

And behold, the LORD passed by, and a great and strong wind tore into the mountains and broke the rocks in pieces before the LORD, but the LORD was not in the wind; and after the wind an earthquake, but the LORD was not in the earthquake; and after the earthquake a fire, but the LORD was not in the fire; and after the fire a still small voice.

I KINGS 19:11–12 (NKJV)

PRAYER

Quiet yourself before the Lord. Listen with your heart and He will comfort and restore; listen for the still small voice that will lead you.

Fear Not

Fear not for I am with you,
Fear not for I am with you,
Fear not for I am with you,
Says the Lord.
I have redeemed you,
I have called you by name,
Child you are Mine.
When you walk through the waters,
I will be there,
And through the flame, you'll not,
no way, be drowned.
You'll not, no way, be burned
For I am with you.

—PHIL PRINGLE

When I tuck my daughters into their beds at night, they inevitably ask that I leave on the night-light. I know their fears are unfounded, but they still need the comfort of a softly glowing light. So I leave the little light shining.

After all, I know what it's like to feel afraid. Even when I know my fears are irrational—like being afraid of the dark—I can't help but feel afraid. Sometimes, however, my fears are well-founded indeed—such as when a loved one faced a difficult medical diagnosis or a tough situation at work made the future look bleak.

Unfounded or not, God has an answer for our fears. His answer is that we "fear not." Easy for Him to say, perhaps, but He also tells us why we can do that: "For I am with you." He has promised to always be with us, His children, whom He has called by name. The darkness may be terrifying, but He will be there, shining a light to guide us on our way. The diagnosis may be grim, but He will strengthen and help us. He will be there with us through it all.

Fear not! He has redeemed us from the grave and has promised us everlasting life. When we come to the end of our rope, He will catch us. And when we come to the end of our lives, He will greet us and welcome us into glory and say, "Child, you are Mine."

Fear not, for I am with you; be not dismayed, for I am your God. I will strengthen you, yes, I will help you, I will uphold you with My righteous right hand.

ISAIAH 41:10 (NKJV)

PRAYER

Cast your fears before Him. Pray that He will give you the courage to face the circumstances of your life and thank Him for being by your side, for promising to be with you always.

High and Exalted

He is high and exalted and worthy of praise
With our hearts we will love and adore.
He is high and exalted and worthy of praise,
Holy is the Lord,
Holy, holy,
Holy is the Lord.

—KYLE RASMUSSEN

*W*ho is in charge of your life? As Christians, we should allow the most high and exalted God to rule our hearts and guide our thoughts and desires. When we attempt to control our lives, we remove God from the highest place—the throne of our hearts.

Yet it can be so difficult to give God control. We want to see results; we want to step in and affect our destiny; we want to make sure that our needs are met. We're not quite sure this invisible God is concerned about every aspect of our lives. We don't want to bother Him with our needs—especially since we think we're perfectly capable of figuring things out on our own.

While God has given us brains to use, we should always keep in those brains the reality of God's rule in our lives. When we give God His rightful place—high and exalted—the Bible promises that we will "lack nothing" (Psalm 34:9). This is not to say we will get whatever we want whenever we want it. On the contrary, God knows that what we want may be detrimental to us, or that right now isn't the best time for us to have it. Instead, we will never lack what we *need*.

So exalt God in your life. Place Him at the very center of every activity, every decision, every joy, every sorrow, and every need. After all, that's right where He wants to be.

The LORD is exalted, for he dwells on high.

ISAIAH 33:5

PRAYER

Ask the Lord to take charge of your life. Give Him the throne of your heart and exalt Him on high.

God Is the Strength of My Heart

Whom have I in Heaven but You?
There is nothing on earth I desire beside You.
My heart and my strength, many times they fail,
But there is one truth that always will prevail.
God is the strength of my heart,
And my portion forever.

—EUGENE GRECO

*G*o get your Bible and take the time to read Psalm 73 all the way through. Many people have found the words there to be very comforting—describing exactly how they have felt at one time or another.

The psalmist tells of the struggles within his heart and mind. He can't understand why those who are wicked are also prosperous. He asks if God knows what is going on down here! In verse 13, he wonders if he's been wasting his time living a life of purity. Indeed, it is hard to understand (or accept!) the prosperity of those who hate the Lord.

But then one day the answer comes to him when he is at prayer. The riches those evil people have exist in this life only. What the psalmist has—what we as Christians have—are riches that will last for eternity. Because we love the Lord, He will guide us all our lives, and afterwards, He will welcome us into the glories of heaven (73:23–24).

Our health may fail, our spirits may droop, and our bank account may be slim, but God remains with us through everything. God is the strength of our hearts. Get as close to Him as you can! It is good to be near the One who remains forever.

My flesh and my heart may fail, but God is the strength of my heart and my portion forever.

PSALM 73:26

PRAYER

Thank the Lord for loving you, for holding your hand, and for giving you strength. Praise Him for His presence in your life forever.

In Your Presence, O God

In Your presence, that's where I am strong,
In Your presence, O Lord, my God,
In Your presence that's where I belong.
Seeking Your face, touching Your grace,
In the cleft of the rock, in Your presence, O God.
I want to go where the rivers cannot overflow me,
Where my feet are on the rock.
I want to hide where the blazing fire cannot burn me
In Your presence, O God.
I want to hide where the flood of evil cannot reach me,
Where I am covered by the blood.
I want to be where the schemes of darkness
cannot touch me,
In Your presence, O God.
You are my firm foundation, I trust in You all day long.
I am Your child and Your servant
And You are my strength and my song.
You're my song.

—LYNN DESHAZO

*I*n your presence, O God, that's where we want to be. Yet how do we get into the presence of God? How do we know if we're there?

The fact is, because we are His children and because He loves us, we could not get out of His presence even if we tried. He is with us always.

However, when we run into trouble, we often think that God has left us. We forget that we are constantly in His presence and can trust in His help. When we are weak or scared, we can run to the Rock. When we go through deep waters, we will not drown. When we try to keep our balance in the currents of difficulty, we will not be swept away! When we walk through the fires of oppression, we will not be consumed by the flames.

God is our firm foundation. Even if all of the powers of darkness swirl around us, we are safe. In His presence we are secure. He has called us His own children, and like a loving parent, He is there to comfort and to guide us.

Call upon Him. Enter His presence with joy! In His presence find strength, comfort, joy, safety, and a song that will fill your heart with praise. In His presence is where you belong!

Fear not, for I have redeemed you; I have summoned you by name; you are mine. When you pass through the waters, I will be with you; and when you pass through the rivers, they will not sweep over you. When you walk through the fire, you will not be burned; the flames will not set you ablaze.

ISAIAH 43:1–2

PRAYER

Ask the Lord to help you with the problems that seem to overwhelm you. Seek His strength, His wisdom, and His power, and then rest in His presence.

I Am the God That Healeth Thee

I am the God that healeth thee,

I am the Lord, your Healer.

I sent My Word and healed your disease,

I am the Lord, your Healer.

You are the God that healeth me,

You are the Lord, my Healer.

You sent Your Word and healed my disease,

You are the Lord, my Healer.

—DON MOEN

*S*he sat in a wheelchair and prayed with all her might. Someone had told her that if she just had "enough faith," she would be able to get up and walk. But try as she might, she remained seated. What of God's promise to heal? The Bible is full of accounts of the healing power of God. When Jesus walked the earth, people were healed by His touch. Why wouldn't He touch her?

The young woman's name is Joni Eareckson Tada, whose story is well known to many. A quadriplegic from a diving accident, she became a believer and prayed to be healed. But God had other plans for this marvelous young woman. He began to use her—wheelchair and all—in a worldwide ministry.

When we pray for healing, for ourselves or for those we love, we must remember to pray that God's will be done. Sometimes physical or mental pain will remain no matter how much we ask God to remove it. Living with afflictions often puts believers in the path of others who deal with the same struggles, providing the opportunity to be witnesses for Him.

And what of the promise? Healing has come—for we have been spiritually healed by His death on our behalf. And physical healing will indeed come. When we enter the gates of heaven, we will all be completely healed. Praise the Lord for His healing power!

Praise the LORD, O my soul, and forget not all his benefits—who forgives all your sins and heals all your diseases. . . . He himself bore our sins in his body on the tree, so that we might die to sins and live for righteousness; by his wounds you have been healed.

PSALM 103:2–3, 1 PETER 2:24

PRAYER

If you're praying for healing today—for yourself or for someone you love—humbly ask God to do His will. Ask Him to give you the courage to accept His plans—whether that includes immediate healing or not.

Our Heart

Our heart, our desire, is to see the nations worship,
Our cry, our prayer is to sing Your praise to the
ends of the earth,
That with one mighty voice, every tribe and tongue rejoices,
Our heart, our desire is to see the nations worship You.
Heavenly Father, Your mercy showers down
upon Your people,
Every race upon the earth.
May Your Spirit pierce the darkness,
break the chains of death upon us,
Let us rise in honest worship to declare
Your matchless worth.
There is no power that for one hour can
withstand Your greatness
Of Your Word, and tongues of faith,
So with bold intercession, claiming all of Your possession,
Praying now that every heart bow before You, Lord, in praise.

—JOHN CHISUM AND GEORGE SEARCY

*I*f our desire really is to see the nations—every race upon the earth—worship the Lord, then we must put that desire into action.

Before Jesus ascended into heaven, He told His disciples to go into all the world and teach others about Himself. Because of the faithfulness of the disciples and those whom they taught and baptized, we know about Jesus today. If the story had not been written down and passed on from one person to the next, from generation to generation, those alive today would not know of the Son of God who came to save us.

Therefore, we must continue to spread the good news. Let us rise in honest worship and declare His matchless worth! Let us share with our family, friends, neighbors, and co-workers the goodness of God—that He came to save us from our sin and break the chains of death. Let us be bold as we intercede for others, claiming His promise.

No power can withstand the greatness of God. When we share His glory, our desire to bring others into the family of God will become active. We will reach all nations and His name will be praised among all peoples of the world.

Send your heart, your prayers, your treasure, and even your very own feet out into the lost world. The Bible asks, "How can they hear without someone preaching to them?" (Romans 10:14). Is that "someone" you?

Therefore go and make disciples of all nations, baptizing them in the name of the Father and of the Son and of the Holy Spirit, and teaching them to obey everything I have commanded you. And surely I am with you always, to the very end of the age.

MATTHEW 28:19–20

PRAYER

Pray that the Lord will make you bold—that your desire to share the good news of His salvation will become action so that others may be led into the family of God.

Can't Stop Talking

Can't stop talking about everything He's done,
It's the best thing to happen since the world begun.
It didn't come cheap, but I got it for free,
It's the hope of glory, Christ in me.
He helped me to see when my spirit was blind,
It's amazing if you look just what you'll find.
Every step I took, He took two,
If He did it for me, He can do it for you.
Do you know Him? Yes I do.
Do you know what I say is true?
Do you know Him? Yes I do.
If He did it for me, He can do it for you.

—RUSSELL FRAGAR

*T*here's nothing like an excited new Christian! Someone who has just experienced the joy of being set free from sin has an infectious spirit—he just can't stop talking about what Jesus has done for him.

The Bible tells us the story of a man who was so thankful for what Jesus had done for Him that he immediately went out and told people about his experience. The man is not named in Scripture, but he could represent any one of us. He was beyond all human help, yet Jesus set him free. The man was so thankful, he begged Jesus to be allowed to join Him. But Jesus sent the man back to his own hometown to share what had happened to him. So the man told everyone about the great things Jesus had done for him, and people were awestruck by his story (Mark 5:1–20).

What is your salvation story? Can you boil it down to three minutes and have it ready to tell at a moment's notice? The apostle Peter advises, "Always be prepared to give an answer to everyone who asks you to give the reason for the hope that you have" (1 Peter 3:15).

If someone asked you about your faith, what would you say about the hope that you have?

Jesus did not let him, but said, "Go home to your family and tell them how much the Lord has done for you, and how he has had mercy on you."

MARK 5:19

PRAYER

Think about your story. Write it down. Say it to yourself. Then ask the Lord to give you opportunities to share the joy of your faith with others.

Can You Believe

Can you believe what the Lord
has done in me?
Can you believe what the Lord
has done in me?
He saved me, cleansed me,
Turned my life around,
Set my feet upon the solid ground.
Can you believe what the Lord
has done in me?

—ALVIN MIRANDA

*S*ometimes joy surprises us—it catches us off guard. When we think about what the Lord has done for us, it's hard to grasp. We get a "can you believe this?" feeling inside.

What God did to save our souls is beyond our ability to comprehend. God, the Creator of the heavens and the earth, loved us so much that He sent His one and only Son to earth. While here, Jesus taught the multitudes about repentance, forgiveness, and love. Then Jesus allowed Himself to be sacrificed for our sins and died a horrible death. He did this willingly. "God demonstrates his own love for us in this: While we were still sinners, Christ died for us" (Romans 5:8).

Not only has He done great things *for* us, but He also does great things *in* us. He cleanses us from sin and forgives every wrongdoing in our past. He turns our lives around so we understand how to live a new life and not repeat the mistakes of the past. He lifts us out of the shifting sands of fear, doubt, and worry and sets our feet upon the solid rock of faith.

Sometimes it's hard to believe what He did for us and in us, but we only need to take a look in the mirror and know it is real. Praise the Lord for surprising us with the joy of His salvation!

But if we are living in the light of God's presence, just as Christ is, then we have fellowship with each other, and the blood of Jesus, his Son, cleanses us from every sin.

1 JOHN 1:7 (NLT)

PRAYER

Thank the Lord for all He has done for you, and for giving you the joy of His salvation. Take a moment to consider what a privilege it is to have been saved by Him.

Thou Art Worthy Great Jehovah

Thou art worthy, great Jehovah,
Thou are worthy, mighty God,
Thou art worthy, Abba Father,
Thou art worthy, Lamb of God.
You are worthy, great Jehovah,
You are worthy, mighty God,
You are worthy, Abba Father,
You are worthy, Lamb of God.

—KAREN CHANDLER EAGAN

*T*o be *worthy* means to be of great value. When we look at what we hold dear, we need to keep Jesus at the top of that list.

He is worthy of praise (2 Samuel 22:4)—praise that comes from those who value Him above all that this world holds dear. He is worthy to receive all glory, honor, and power (Revelation 4:11) because He is the Creator and Sustainer of everything. He is worthy to break the seals and open the scroll that contains God's plan for the world (Revelation 5:5). He is the only one worthy to do this because He is the only person to ever live a perfect, sinless life. He died for the sins of the world and then showed His power over sin and death by rising from the grave!

Because of His sacrifice, those who love Him are also worthy! He makes us worthy to enter the kingdom of heaven by presenting us with the gift of salvation. "For He has rescued us from the dominion of darkness and brought us into the kingdom of the Son He loves, in whom we have redemption, the forgiveness of sin" (Colossians 1:13–14). And Paul encourages us, "Live a life worthy of the calling you have received" (Ephesians 4:1).

Because He is worthy, we as His heirs are also worthy. Abba, Father, You are worthy!

Worthy is the Lamb, who was slain, to receive power and wealth and wisdom and strength and honor and glory and praise!

REVELATION 5:12

PRAYER

Thank God for the worthiness you have received in Christ. Ask Him to help you to hold Him up in the most valuable and honored place in your life.

Take Me In

Take me past the outer court and through
the holy place,
Past the brazen altar, Lord, I want to
see Your face.
Pass me by the crowds of people
And the priests who sing their praise.
Lord, I hunger and thirst for Your righteousness
But it's only found in one place.
So take me in to the Holy of Holies
Take me in by the blood of the Lamb,
So take me in to the Holy of Holies
Take the coal, cleanse my lips,
Here I am.

—DAVID BROWNING

*I*n the Old Testament, the most holy place of the temple, the holy of holies, was to be entered only by the high priest, and only once a year in order to sacrifice and atone for the sins of the people (Leviticus 16). God Himself was present there.

God had given very strict rules regarding entrance into the holy of holies. The high priest was to throw handfuls of incense onto a fire, producing a cloud that would obscure any view of God. If anyone looked into the holy of holies, he would die.

But the death of Jesus changed the rules. In fact, at the very moment when His life ended on the cross, the curtain separating the holy of holies from the rest of the temple was torn in two from top to bottom (Matthew 27:51). From that moment on, the barrier between sinful humanity and the holy God was removed.

Where the high priests had to spend hours preparing to enter the presence of the Lord, we can meet God any time, any place. Whenever we desire to see His face, whenever we hunger and thirst for His righteousness, we need only to call out to Him. The blood was shed by the Lamb of God and we are now welcomed into the holy of holies—the presence of the Lord.

Blessed are those who hunger and thirst for righteousness, for they will be filled.

MATTHEW 5:6

PRAYER

Draw near to the holy of holies in prayer. Ask the Lord to lead you as you seek His righteousness.

Eagle's Wings

Here I am waiting,

Abide in me, I pray.

Here I am longing for You.

Hide me in Your love,

Bring me to my knees,

May I know Jesus

More and more.

Come live in me

All my life take over,

Come breathe in me

And I will rise on eagle's wings.

—REUBEN MORGAN

*M*uch has been written about the legendary "fountain of youth"—a place where one could sip luscious water and stay young, healthy, and vibrant even into old age.

Who doesn't want to stay young? As we age, we bemoan our aching muscles, our wrinkles, our health issues, our waning strength. We long for the days when we thought we could take on the world. Now we only hope to stay healthy through the long winter.

You know, there's nothing wrong with aging. In fact, the Bible sees it as a great blessing. Proverbs 16:31 says, "Gray hair is a crown of splendor." Psalm 71:18 records the prayer of one who is old and gray as he desires to declare God's power to the next generation. The Bible acknowledges the changes of old age but honors the wisdom and experience that replace the strength and vigor of youth.

If you're among the aged today, honor God with your experience and your wisdom. Pass along your faith to the next generation. Despite the aches and pains of your aging body, you can have your youth renewed by continuing to do the work God still calls you to do.

If you're still among the youthful, thank God for your health. Serve Him with your vigor. In addition, honor the wise older believers in your family and at your church. Ask them about their faith; encourage them to share what God has done for them. Then be ready to listen!

Praise the Lord, O my soul . . . who satisfies your desires with good things so that your youth is renewed like the eagle's.

PSALM 103:2, 5

PRAYER

Talk to the Lord about your age. Ask Him to teach you how to be His servant no matter how old or young you are.

In Your Presence

In Your presence there is fullness of joy,
At Your right hand there are
pleasures evermore.
You surround us with Your favor, O Lord,
The earth is full of Your goodness.
The earth is filled with Your love.
Exceedingly, abundantly,
Far above all we
Could ever ask or think,
Exceedingly, abundantly,
You give us all things to enjoy.

—BILLY FUNK AND MARTIN J. NYSTROM

xceeding—to go beyond the limits. Abundance—a plentiful or overflowing supply.

In His presence, we find an exceeding abundance of joy. So much that we cannot begin to take it in. He surrounds us with limitless love, mercy, and forgiveness. The earth is plentiful and supplies all of our needs. In His goodness and love He created all that we enjoy from the earth.

What more could we ask for? He has provided for us exceedingly and abundantly. And then, on top of that, He tells us to *enjoy* them.

So enjoy! Take in the sunset. Feel the wind whipping through your hair. Marvel at the smile of your child. Revel in the sweetness of a blueberry pie. Let your feet sink into the sand and let the waves lap at your legs. Smell the luscious aroma of a rose. Hug your friends. Laugh at the good jokes. Thank the Lord for all in life that He has given you to enjoy—and *enjoy!*

Now to Him who is able to do exceedingly abundantly above all that we ask or think, according to the power that works in us, to Him be glory in the church by Christ Jesus to all generations, forever and ever. Amen.

EPHESIANS 3:20–21 (NKJV)

PRAYER

Thank the Lord for filling you with joy and surrounding you with His goodness exceedingly and abundantly.

Such Joy

Such joy, such unspeakable joy,
Such peace, an everlasting peace,
Such love, a pure and holy love,
Spirit have Your way in me.
There's a peace that floods my soul
When the Spirit of the Lord is in control.
There's a joy no bounds can hold
When the Spirit blows a fresh wind
through my soul.
Holy Spirit flow through me,
Touch my heart and there will
There will be.

—DON HARRIS

*S*ometimes we just wish we could control everything around us. Control our spouse, control our kids, control our boss, control our physical bodies, control our church, control the world! If we could just be put in charge, we could make everything just right. But give us that much control and we'd soon find ourselves in a big mess— out of control.

Without Christ in our lives, however, we are left with way too much to try to control. Imagine having to make the big decisions of life without any recourse except the advice of friends and our own limited understanding and knowledge. Contrast that with our being able to talk to the God of the universe who knows the future, who loves us, and promises to guide us. Suddenly being in control doesn't seem quite so important.

What we need, instead, is Spirit-control. And as the song says, "There's a peace that floods my soul when the Spirit of the Lord is in control." Like a stuffy room in which the windows are thrown open to let in the spring air, the Spirit blows a fresh wind through our souls. When we open our hands and release control of our lives, He brings His unspeakable joy, everlasting peace, and pure and holy love.

So don't seek to be in control; seek to have Spirit-control. You'll find your greatest peace when you let go and let God.

Though you have not seen him, you love him; and even though you do not see him now, you believe in him and are filled with an inexpressible and glorious joy.

1 PETER 1:8

PRAYER

Ask the Lord to help you identify the areas of your life where you feel the need to control. Then let go of them—give them over to Him.

He Is the King of Kings

He is the King of kings,
He is the Lord of lords,
His name is Jesus,
Jesus, Jesus, Jesus,
Oh, He is the King.

—VIRGIL MEARS

*J*esus is often referred to as our friend, our brother, and our Savior. While He is all of these, He is also a King—*the* King— and we must not forget the importance of that title.

The word *king* brings many visions to the mind's eye. A king is responsible for his nation. A king sits in judgment over the deeds of others. A king protects his people from invaders. A king solves the problems of his people. A king is powerful and mighty.

Where many kings on earth, in the past and today, failed miserably at one or more of their responsibilities, we know that there is one King who will live up to all of the expectations we can place upon kingship. That is why He is called "King of kings."

Our King will never let us down. He is always there to guard our hearts, protecting us from attempted invasions by the armies of Satan. He judges us by the law, but is always willing to forgive us when we ask. Our King exudes power and might. No one is powerful enough to stand against Him.

Praise the Lord that we can approach the throne of the King and know that He will always forgive our sins and protect us from evil. He is the King of kings!

God, the blessed and only Ruler, the King of kings and Lord of lords, who alone is immortal and who lives in unapproachable light, whom no one has seen or can see. To him be honor and might forever. Amen.

1 TIMOTHY 6:15–16

PRAYER

Thank Jesus for being more than a brother, more than a friend—thank Him for being your Savior and King.

Rejoice for the Steps

Rejoice for the steps of a righteous man,
They are ordered of God, they are
ordered of God.
Rejoice for the steps of a righteous man,
They are ordered of God.
In the time of trouble, God will uphold him,
God will preserve him, God will sustain him,
In the time of trouble, God will lift him up,
So rejoice, those steps are ordered of God.

—HENRY GASKINS

*I*magine taking a long journey without a map. We wouldn't dream of just getting on the road, driving aimlessly, and hoping to get to our destination. Instead, we follow the map and watch for the right crossroads. If we get lost, we can search the map and get back on track.

As Christians, we're all on the road of life taking our different paths. Some of us will take a more scenic route, some of us will find ourselves driving through deserts, others are in the mountains. But we all have the same destination—we're seeking to obey God and become more like Christ. So we need to follow a map—and that map is God's Word. The Bible contains directions for the journey of life. Sometimes we're too proud to ask for directions or we decide we want to go our own way. Then, when we are hopelessly lost, miles from the nearest paved road . . . and the rain begins . . . suddenly we realize that if we had just consulted the map, we wouldn't be in such a jam.

Are you lost today? Not sure where you're going? The steps of righteous people are ordered of God. Check out the map and follow the directions daily. When you do, you're sure to reach your destination.

The steps of the godly are directed by the LORD. He delights in every detail of their lives.

PSALM 37:23 (NLT)

PRAYER

Ask the Lord for His guidance. Pray that He will uphold, preserve, and sustain you as you follow His direction for your life.

The Name of the Lord

Oh the name of the Lord,

it's like a strong tower,

The righteous shall run unto it and be glad.

Oh the name of the Lord,

it's like a strong tower,

The righteous shall run unto it.

They'll go forth in victory,

Triumphing over the enemy,

Yes, they'll go forth

To kick in the gates of hell,

For they are the army of God,

For they are the army of God.

—CURTIS PEIFER

*D*ifferent towers are built for different purposes. Some are for keeping watch, such as the fire towers that stand throughout America's national forests. Other towers are for providing a point of reference on a landscape, such as the lighthouses that dot the shores of our oceans and the Great Lakes.

These towers are necessary for the safety of many people. Without them fires would go unnoticed until they burn uncontrollably; ships would be lost or would run aground without the light to guide them.

It is no coincidence, then, that the Lord is compared to a tower. In ancient times, towers were placed on the corners of walled cities. Lookouts could see great distances and warn the people inside the city when an unfriendly army was approaching. Those outside the city would have time to find safety within the walls, even as the army of that city could be assembled for battle.

The Lord is our tower—the place to which we run when we need protection, the light that guides us through the darkness. Then, when we've seen the advancing enemy, we can burst forth from the tower and claim victory, as only the army of the Lord can do!

The name of the LORD is a strong tower; the righteous run to it and are safe.

PROVERBS 18:10

PRAYER

Thank the Lord for being your place of refuge, the strong tower to which you can run and prepare to do battle. Ask Him to guide you to victory.

From the Rising of the Sun

From the rising of the sun
To the going down of the same,
The Lord's name is to be praised.
Praise ye the Lord.
Praise Him all ye servants of the Lord.
Praise the name of the Lord,
Blessed be the name of the Lord
From this time forth and forevermore.

—PAUL DEMING

ur days are hectic—full of appointments, tasks, and dead-lines—from the rising of the sun to the going down of the same. From the moment we roll out of bed in the morning until we roll back in at night, we are on the go. How in the world are we to find time to praise?

Yet the author of this psalm reminds us that we must praise God all day long. Now and then won't suffice. From the rising of the sun to when it sets—that's all day long—the Lord's name is to be praised. When we keep our minds focused on Him, the day will go more smoothly. When we remember to praise Him for the things He has done for us and for what He has given us, complaining and griping don't have a chance!

Begin the day with praise. Thank the Lord for another day in which to live and work, to spend time with family and friends, to share His love. Praise Him all the day long for everything from the minute (an empty parking space near the front door) to the grand (a loved one recovering from an illness). Let His praises permeate your thoughts, words, and actions.

Praise the Lord from this time forth, and forevermore!

Blessed be the name of the LORD from this time forth and for evermore. From the rising of the sun unto the going down of the same the LORD's name is to be praised.

PSALM 113:2−3 (KJV)

PRAYER

Ask the Lord to make Himself evident to you throughout the day that you may begin to build a habit of praising Him all day long.

DAY 80

I See the Lord

I see the Lord and He is seated
on the throne
The train of His robe is filling the heavens.
I see the Lord and He is shining like the sun
His eyes full of fire, His voice
like the waters.
Surrounding His throne are
thousands singing,
Holy, holy, holy
Is the Lord God Almighty.
Holy, holy, holy
Is the Lord.

—PAUL BALOCHE

There is so much about God that we don't know. The Bible gives us an amazing account of everything He has done, from the creation of the world to the life, death, and resurrection of Jesus. We even have a glimpse into the future. The Bible gives us so much, and yet our view of God is still hazy and blurred. Our human minds cannot comprehend His glory.

How awesome, then, is the thought that someday we will see Him face to face. He will be seated on the throne of heaven and will appear in all His majesty and power. Revelation 4 describes how beautiful, and yet how terrifying, the throne room of God will be. His throne is made of precious gems and from it come flashes of lightning and the rumble of thunder.

The train of His robe fills the heavens. His eyes are full of fire, He shines like the sun. His voice is like the waters. Can you picture it? Can you hear it? Even the greatest artist could not do this scene justice. For now, we are bound by human experience. Then, we will see heaven with new eyes and everything will be made clear.

Join with the thousands in singing, "Holy, holy, holy is the Lord God Almighty." His splendor is magnificent beyond imagination. But, praise be to God, someday we will see Him face to face.

In the same way, we can see and understand only a little about God now, as if we were peering at His reflection in a poor mirror, but someday we are going to see Him in his completeness, face to face. Now all that I know is hazy and blurred, but then I will see everything clearly, just as clearly as God sees into my heart right now.

1 CORINTHIANS 13:12 (TLB)

PRAYER

Meditate on God's holiness. Think about His beauty and power. Try to picture in your mind what it will one day be like to stand face to face with your Savior and Lord.

Let God Arise

Let God arise, let God arise,

Let God arise, let God arise.

Let His enemies be scattered

And let the righteous be glad.

Yes, let them rejoice with gladness,

God has triumphed mightily.

—JOHN SELLERS

*S*ometimes we become so wrapped up in what we don't have that we forget all of the blessings we do have. When a job is hard to find or we don't have the money for the little extras that we think will make us happy, we become unhappy, maybe even angry or jealous of those who have more.

Discontent, anger, and jealousy . . . these are the enemies of joy. It is difficult to be happy—to rejoice in the Lord—when those enemies invade our hearts. We need to be content and thankful with what we have been blessed with. The high profile job might not be ours, but we will be able to pay the bills and provide for our family's basic needs by waiting tables. We might not be able to pay for summer camp, but we can spend time with our family at the local park. Others may have more *things* than us, but are *things* really that important?

Let God arise in your heart and mind and remove the enemies that drive away your joy. Be thankful for all He has given you—His love, forgiveness, and eternal life. You may not have all of the physical things you desire, but those things will pass away. The love of family, friends, and your Savior is eternal.

May God arise, may his enemies be scattered; may his foes flee before him. . . . Sing to God, sing praise to his name, extol him who rides on the clouds—his name is the LORD— and rejoice before him.

PSALM 68:1, 4

PRAYER

Think about the many blessings you have received from God. Thank Him and ask Him to help you to be content with all you have been given.

God Is My Refuge

God is my refuge

And God is my strength,

A very present help in trouble.

Therefore I will not fear

Though the earth be removed

And though the mountains

Be carried into the midst of the sea.

—JUDY HORNER MONTEMAYOR

The future. What will happen tomorrow, next week, or a decade down the road is anybody's guess. But not knowing shouldn't upset Christians. God knows our fears, but more importantly, God knows our future.

God will never give you more than you can handle. Therefore, you can trust that God will give you a future that will be fit for you. The future may not be easy or pleasant, but God will give you the strength to endure any trial.

The Living Bible puts it this way: "We need not fear even if the world blows up, and the mountains crumble into the sea. . . . The Commander of the heavenly armies is here among us. He, the God of Jacob, has come to rescue us!" (Psalm 46:2, 11). What a promise! We need not fear even the utter destruction of the earth. God is our refuge! God is our strength!

Whatever the future may hold—a new job, moving to a new town, the loss of people or things you hold dear—never forget that God is your refuge and strength. When you are in trouble, when you begin to fear what lies ahead, trust in His unfailing love for you. His blessings and promises run deeper than any trial.

God is our refuge and strength, an ever-present help in trouble. Therefore we will not fear, though the earth give way and the mountains fall into the heart of the sea.

PSALM 46:1–2

PRAYER

Come before the Lord with your fears about the future. Ask Him to remind you to run to the refuge of His love whenever you face doubt or uncertainty. He is your ever-present help in troubled times.

Make a Joyful Noise

Make a joyful noise unto the Lord,

For He is worthy to be praised,

Sing with your spirit,

Clap with your hands,

Our God is greatly to be praised.

Worthy, worthy, He is worthy to be praised.

Hallelujah!

Our God is greatly to be praised.

—RUSSELL LOWE

When my three daughters are playing together—at least in those moments when they're all getting along—the cacophony brings laughter to my heart. It is indeed a joyful noise! In fact, I worry most when it is quiet. That surely means trouble is afoot. When my oldest daughter (then age six) used her daddy's beard trimmer to cut her sister's (age four) hair, it was indeed very quiet—at least until *I* discovered what had happened!

God loves our joyful noise! He loves it when we sing and clap our hands. Of course the times of quiet are good for our souls, but so are the times when rejoicing bubbles to the top of our spirits and we can't help but declare the goodness of God and the attributes of His character.

Sure, we can sing along with the worship leader on Sunday morning or with the CD in the car stereo. But when the song of praise reaches into our souls and lifts us to the Rock that is higher, we can enter into fellowship with God. We worship not just with our mouths, but with our whole beings. The joyful noise coming from the hearts of His people is evidence of our gratefulness for all He has done for us. Don't stay quiet. Make a joyful noise unto the Lord!

Sing to the LORD, all the earth; proclaim his salvation day after day. Declare his glory among the nations, his marvelous deeds among all peoples. For great is the LORD and most worthy of praise; he is to be feared above all gods.

1 CHRONICLES 16:23–25

PRAYER

Give thanks to God for bringing joy to your life. Praise Him with your whole heart and ask for His blessing upon you.

Hallelujah to the Lamb

Hallelujah, hallelujah, hallelujah to the Lamb.
Hallelujah, hallelujah, by the blood of Christ we stand.
Every tongue, every tribe, every people, every land,
Giving glory, giving honor, giving praise unto
the Lamb of God.
Lord, I stand in the midst of a multitude
Of those from every tribe and tongue.
We are Your people, redeemed by Your blood,
Rescued from death by Your love.
There are no words good enough to thank You.
There are no words to express my praise.
But I will lift up my voice and sing from my heart
With all of my strength.
Every knee shall bow, every tongue confess that
You are Lord of all.
Giving praise unto the Lamb of God,
Jesus Christ, Lamb of God.

—DEBBIE GRAAFSMA AND DON MOEN

I don't generally like crowds. Living on Long Island gives us ample opportunity to visit the wonders and excitement of New York City, but besides the annual anniversary celebration, my husband and I don't often make the trip. Some people are energized by crowds; we prefer the quiet and solitude of the seashore.

There is one crowd I'm looking forward to joining, however, and this song sings about it. I look forward to standing in the midst of the multitude of believers from all over the world as we bow before our Savior!

We are His people, redeemed by His blood. We will stand with the multitude, with Christians from every tribe and every nation, praising God in every language. We who were rescued from death will lift our voices in thanks to our Lord and Savior. What an awesome chorus that will be! I love to sing—and I can hardly wait to sing with that multitude and all the angels of heaven, giving praise to Jesus Christ, the Lamb of God.

Hallelujah to the Lamb! He is worthy to be praised, our Lamb of God, our Rescuer, our Redeemer. Give Him the praise forever and ever!

After this I looked and there before me was a great multitude that no one could count, from every nation, tribe, people and language, standing before the throne and in front of the Lamb. They were wearing white robes and were holding palm branches in their hands. And they cried out in a loud voice: "Salvation belongs to our God, who sits on the throne, and to the Lamb."

REVELATION 7:9–10

PRAYER

If you have not done so before now, bow before Him and confess your sins. Thank Him for being your sacrifice and accept His gift of grace and lordship of your life. Then you can join that glorious multitude in heaven!

Jesus You Are Welcome

Jesus, You are welcome here,

Jesus, You are welcome here,

When Your people praise You,

You said You'd draw near.

Let our worship tell You,

You are welcome here.

Gathered in this place, Lord,

Your name we're gonna bless.

You are welcome here, You are welcome here.

Fill us with Your presence,

Lord, be our special guest.

Come oh Jesus, You are welcome here.

—GERON DAVIS

There are certain things we do—and don't do—when we are expecting guests. Most of us try to tidy up our home, maybe even dust the furniture and sweep the floors. If the guests are staying for an extended period, we give them a room in our home with fresh linens on the bed. But most importantly, we make them feel welcome.

When we attend church, we attempt to make each other feel welcome; we extend a greeting to visitors; we catch up with our friends. The church is like a home to us with a big extended family. We feel welcome, and we in turn seek to make others feel welcome.

But does Jesus feel welcome there? Have we noted His presence with us? Have we entered His place of worship and invited Him to join us there? After all, we have gathered to worship Him. He is the special guest who sits in every pew, speaks to every heart, and listens to the praises of each one of us.

Enter your church service with an open heart, inviting Jesus to fill you with His presence. Remember to welcome Him into your heart and into your worship. Give Him the honor of a special guest and tell Him that you welcome His presence. Then join with the rest of your family and friends as you bless His holy name!

As God has said: "I will live with them and walk among them, and I will be their God, and they will be my people."

2 CORINTHIANS 6:16

PRAYER

Invite Jesus to be your honored guest in your heart—tell Him He is welcome there.

Every Move I Make

Every move I make I make in You,

You make me move Jesus,

Every breath I take I breathe in You.

Every step I take I take in You,

You are my way, Jesus,

Every breath I take, I breathe in You.

Waves of mercy, waves of grace,

Everywhere I look, I see Your face.

Your love has captured me,

Oh my God, this love, how can it be.

—DAVID RUIS

My husband is an avid runner. Not your run-of-the-mill type runner. No, he's the every day, on the road, marathon-training sort of runner. He also teaches about physical training. He'll be the first to tell you that you need to have a plan. You won't be able to do a few stretches at the starting line of a marathon and think that, without training, you can finish it. You need to learn the mechanics of running, training different muscles, eating right, wearing the right clothing and shoes, and even breathing correctly. In fact, if you're going to be really good, you have to take running and competing to the level of an art form. You must be committed to the running "lifestyle."

You see, our bodies are amazing. The more I learn, the more I'm amazed at what intricate creatures we are. We have been created by a loving God—we are not accidents of evolution. When God breathed the breath of life into the first man, the Bible tells us he "became a living being" (Genesis 2:7). We owe our very existence to our Creator. Every move we make, every breath we take is ours because of His loving breath on our lives.

Maybe you won't run a marathon—but you probably have a busy schedule that will keep you running today. Thank the Lord for breath and life. Ask Him to be with you every step of the way. Ask Him to show you how to make that dependence upon Him your lifestyle.

It is God who arms me with strength and makes my way perfect. He makes my feet like the feet of a deer; he enables me to stand on the heights. . . . You broaden the path beneath me, so that my ankles do not turn.

PSALM 18:32–33, 36

PRAYER

Ask the Lord to help you to walk in His way. Commit to learning what it takes to be dependent upon Him every moment of every day, for every breath you take.

We Will Ride

He has fire in His eyes and a sword in His hand,

He's riding a white horse all across this land,

And He's calling out to you and me, "Will you ride with Me?"

And we say, "Yes, Lord, we will ride with You."

And we say, "Yes, Lord, we will stand up and fight."

We will ride with the armies of heaven,

we'll be dressed in white.

He has a crown on His head, He carries a scepter in His hand,

He's leading the armies all across this land.

You see that fire in His eyes is His love for His bride.

And He's longing that she be with Him, right by His side.

Lord, I know what I want my answer to be.

Don't want anything down here holding on to me,

Yes, Lord, yes, Lord.

—ANDY PARK

*I*n the Book of Revelation, Jesus is often referred to as the Lamb—the One who was sacrificed for the sins of all. But when the end draws near, Jesus appears not as a Lamb, but as a warrior on a white horse. He is coming back as a conqueror and King!

Where will your heart be when He returns? Will your heart be His that you may join with the armies of heaven? Will you be taking part in the marriage feast when Jesus calls His bride (the church) to join Him? If your sins were forgiven by the Lamb of God, then your heart belongs to the King of kings, the rider on the white horse.

Christians can look forward to the return of the King because we are His people! But until then, we must take up the sword of truth and be bold in telling others about Jesus. We must be willing to share His love and the way of salvation. We are soldiers in the army of God; we can't afford to go through life acting as if we are not! Those whose lives we touch each day must be given the chance to know Him too. Some will be willing to join with the army of heaven; some will not. But they must be given the choice.

As for us, we can sing out, "Yes, Lord, yes!" We will ride with Him and we will fight the final battle in which all evil will be defeated forever. Hallelujah to the Lamb! Hallelujah to the King!

I saw heaven standing open and there before me was a white horse, whose rider is called Faithful and True. With justice he judges and makes war. . . . The armies of heaven were following him, riding on white horses and dressed in fine linen, white and clean.

REVELATION 19:11, 14

PRAYER

Pray that the Lord will make you a true warrior of faith. Ask that He will make you strong in sharing His salvation with others. Tell Him "yes," you'll ride with Him.

Come into the Holy of Holies

Come into the Holy of Holies,
Enter by the Blood of the Lamb,
Come into His presence with singing,
Worship at the throne of God.
Lifting holy hands
To the King of kings,
Worship Jesus.

—JOHN SELLERS

*T*he holy of holies (also called the Most Holy Place) was a room in the tabernacle, and later in the temple, separated by a curtain. Behind this curtain was the ark of the covenant where God Himself dwelt. This room was to be entered only by the high priest, and then only once a year on the Day of Atonement when he would offer a sacrifice for the sins of the entire nation.

When Jesus became the sacrifice for all, there was no longer the need for a high priest to sacrifice for us. The curtain that had separated the holy of holies was torn in half on the day Jesus died (Matthew 27:51). His shed blood allows all who believe to come into the presence of God at any time—not just once a year.

As believers, we are privileged to have immediate personal access to God through His Son Jesus. No one can come to the Father except through Jesus. The blood of the Lamb has cleansed us and given us the blessing of worshiping before the throne of God. We can now boldly enter the holy of holies and go right into God's presence.

Praise the Creator, Redeemer, King of kings. He has made a way for us and has given us access to God. Join with the redeemed and come into the holy of holies. The blood of the Lamb has made it possible—for you!

And so, dear brothers and sisters, we can boldly enter heaven's Most Holy Place because of the blood of Jesus. . . . Let us go right into the presence of God, with true hearts fully trusting him.

HEBREWS 10:19, 22 (NLT)

PRAYER

Thank God for giving you a way to reach Him through His Son, Jesus Christ. Praise Him for giving you entrance into the holy of holies by covering your sins with the blood of the Lamb.

Let Your Glory Fall

Let Your glory fall, we are thirsty, Lord.

Hear us as we call, fill us now,

Let Your glory fall.

Every tongue and tribe gathered

round Your throne

With one voice we cry, "Holy Lord."

Every tongue and tribe.

Glory to the Lamb, Lamb upon the throne,

All the saints proclaim,

Jesus reigns.

Glory to the Lamb.

—DON MOEN

*W*orship time in church means different things to different people. For some, the singing of beloved hymns accompanied by a pipe organ and a choir is true worship. For others, singing choruses accompanied by a band of musicians with a trumpet, electric guitar, and drum set is the epitome of worship.

Whatever music style you may choose, when your congregation comes together praising the Lord in song, God is there. When we come together in one voice to thank the Lord for what He has done, the glory of the Lord will fill the place, just as it did when Solomon dedicated the temple.

So get involved in your worship time. You are entering a great tradition stretching back through the centuries. Listen carefully to the words. Even if you personally don't like the old hymns or if you can't quite get used to the drumbeat, open your heart to God. Thank Him for songwriters and musicians who put into words praise for God's goodness, love, mercy, forgiveness, and strength.

No matter how you worship, whatever your method of praise, the Lord accepts it all—from the *a cappella* choir to the orchestra. When we unite in thanking and glorifying God, His glory will fall upon us!

The trumpeters and singers joined in unison, as with one voice, to give praise and thanks to the Lord. Accompanied by trumpets, cymbals and other instruments, they raised their voices in praise to the Lord and sang: "He is good; his love endures forever." Then the temple of the Lord was filled with a cloud, and the priests could not perform their service because of the cloud, for the glory of the Lord filled the temple of God.

2 CHRONICLES 5:13-14

PRAYER

Begin your prayer by thanking God, by worshiping His holiness. Then the way will be clear for you to bring your needs and concerns before Him.

We Will Wait

We will run and not grow weary,

We will walk and will not faint,

For the Lord will go before us

And His joy will be our strength.

Mounting up with wings as eagles

As our spirits start to soar.

When we come into His presence

And we wait upon the Lord.

We will wait upon the Lord,

For in His presence is fullness of joy

And our strength will be restored

As we wait upon the Lord.

—TRICIA ALLEN GRANT AND MARTY NYSTROM

*H*istory is filled with the names of people who, even after failing again and again, achieved great successes. Abraham Lincoln, Orville and Wilbur Wright, Albert Einstein, Benjamin Franklin, and Thomas Edison are just the tip of the iceberg. What they all had in common was that they never gave up. They pressed on toward their goals. Their discoveries and inventions are widely known—their failures are largely forgotten.

For Christians, our ultimate goal is life in heaven. While still here on earth, we sometimes become weary. When we see injustices or face persecution, we become weak. It's not always easy to be a Christian.

But God has made us a promise. Our troubles are not hidden from Him. He understands the human condition far deeper than we can comprehend. He is the Creator, the everlasting God, and He never grows tired or weary. No matter how many times we fail, stumble, or fall, if our hope is in the Lord, He *will* renew our strength. That is His promise to us.

Wait upon the Lord. He will give the strength to be witnesses for Him and to face the harsh words of those who don't believe. He will forgive our failures and renew our ability to serve Him. We can accomplish much for Him in the time we have been given. He is faithful to remember our successes and forget our failures. Thanks to Him, we can mount up with wings like eagles, soaring into His presence with joy.

But they that wait upon the Lord shall renew their strength. They shall mount up with wings like eagles; they shall run and not be weary; they shall walk and not faint.

ISAIAH 40:31 (TLB)

PRAYER

Thank the Lord for His promise to renew your strength when you are weary, and for loving you enough to forgive you when you fail.

"Above All Else" by Kirk Dearman and Deby Dearman. © 1988 Integrity's Hosanna! Music/ASCAP. c/o Integrity Media, Inc., 1000 Cody Rd., Mobile, AL 36695.

"Ah, Lord God" by Kay Chance. © 1976 Kay Chance.

"As for Me and My House" by Tom Brooks, Don Harris, and Martin J. Nystrom. © 1994 Integrity's Hosanna! Music. c/o Integrity Media, Inc., 1000 Cody Rd., Mobile, AL 36695.

"Be Magnified" by Lynn DeShazo. © 1992 Integrity's Hosanna! Music/ASCAP. c/o Integrity Media, Inc., 1000 Cody Rd., Mobile, AL 36695.

"Blessed Be the Name of the Lord" by Mark Levang and Cathy Riso. © 1994 Integrity's Hosanna! Music/ASCAP & Integrity's Praise! Music/Mom's Fudge (admin. by Integrity's Praise! Music). BMI. c/o Integrity Media, Inc., 1000 Cody Rd., Mobile, AL 36695.

"Blessed Be the Rock" by Daniel Gardner. © 1985 Integrity's Hosanna! Music/ASCAP. c/o Integrity Media, Inc., 1000 Cody Rd., Mobile, AL 36695.

"Breathe on Me" by Lucy Fisher. © 1998 Lucy Fisher/Hillsong Publishing (admin. in the U.S. and Canada by Integrity's Hosanna! Music)/ASCAP. c/o Integrity Media, Inc., 1000 Cody Rd., Mobile, AL 36695.

"Can You Believe" by Alvin Miranda. © 1996 Bargain Basement Music/ASCAP (admin. by ICG) and Integrity's Hosanna! Music/ASCAP. c/o Integrity Media, Inc., 1000 Cody Rd., Mobile, AL 36695.

"Can't Stop Talking" by Russell Fragar. © 1996 Russell Fragar/Hillsong Publishing (admin. in the U.S. and Canada by Integrity's Hosanna! Music)/ASCAP. c/o Integrity Media, Inc., 1000 Cody Rd., Mobile, AL 36695.

"Change My Heart Oh God" by Ed Kerr. © 1992 Integrity's Hosanna! Music/ASCAP. c/o Integrity Media, Inc., 1000 Cody Rd., Mobile, AL 36695.

"Change My Heart, Oh God" by Eddie Espinosa. © 1982 Mercy/Vineyard Publishing/ASCAP.

"Come into the Holy of Holies" by John Sellers. © 1984 Integrity's Hosanna! Music/ASCAP. c/o Integrity Media, Inc., 1000 Cody Rd., Mobile, AL 36695.

"Days of Elijah" by Robin Mark. © 1996 Daybreak Music Ltd. (admin. in N. & S. America by Integrity's Hosanna! Music)/ASCAP. c/o Integrity Media, Inc., 1000 Cody Rd., Mobile, AL 36695.

"Eagles Wings" by Reuben Morgan. © 1998 Reuben Morgan/Hillsong Publishing (admin. in the U.S. and Canada by Integrity's Hosanna! Music)/ASCAP. c/o Integrity Media, Inc., 1000 Cody Rd., Mobile, AL 36695.

"Every Move I Make" by Davis Ruis. © 1996 Mercy/Vineyard Publishing/Vineyard Songs Canada (admin. by Mercy/Vineyard Publishing in the U.S.)(ASCAP).

"Fear Not" by Phil Pringle. © 1984 Seam of Gold (a division of Christian City Church, Oxford Falls, Sydney, Australia).

"From the Rising of the Sun" by Paul Deming. © 1976 Integrity's Hosanna! Music/ASCAP. c/o Integrity Media, Inc., 1000 Cody Rd., Mobile, AL 36695.

"God Is in the House" by Russell Fragar and Darlene Zschech. © 1996 Russell Fragar (Hillsong Publishing)/Darlene Zschech (Hillsong Publishing) (admin. in the U.S. and Canada by Integrity's Hosanna! Music)/ASCAP. c/o Integrity Media, Inc., 1000 Cody Rd., Mobile, AL 36695.

"God Is My Refuge" by Judy Horner Montemayor. © 1973 Integrity's Hosanna! Music/ASCAP. c/o Integrity Media, Inc., 1000 Cody Rd., Mobile, AL 36695.

"God Is the Strength of My Heart" by Eugene Greco. © 1989 Integrity's Hosanna! Music/ASCAP. c/o Integrity Media, Inc., 1000 Cody Rd., Mobile, AL 36695.

"Hallelujah to the Lamb" by Debbie Graafsma and Don Moen. © 1997 Integrity's Hosanna! Music/ASCAP. c/o Integrity Media, Inc., 1000 Cody Rd., Mobile, AL 36695.

"Hallowed Be Thy Name" by Babbie Mason and Robert Lawson. © 1988 Word Music, Inc./ASCAP. All rights reserved. Used by permission. International copyright secured.

"He Is the King of Kings" by Virgil Mears. © 1989 Integrity's Hosanna! Music. c/o Integrity Media, Inc., 1000 Cody Rd., Mobile, AL 36695.

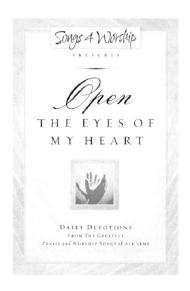

The first book of the series, Open the Eyes of My Heart *is a beautiful daily devotional that will lead you into the presence of God, featuring 90 spiritually-moving devotionals based on the greatest praise and worship songs of all time.* ISBN 1-59145-021-7

The second book of the series, Give Thanks with a Grateful Heart *is a beautiful daily devotional of thanksgiving and love toward God, featuring 90 more spiritually-moving devotionals based on more of the best praise and worship songs of all time.* ISBN 1-59145-022-5

INTEGRITY
P U B L I S H E R S

Available wherever books are sold.

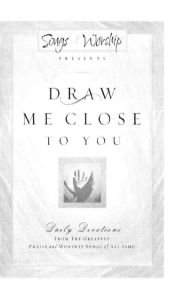

The third book of the series,
Draw Me Close to You *is*
another beautiful daily devotional
that will guide you to draw close
to God even as He draws close to
you, featuring 90 devotionals
based on the inspiring words of
more of the best praise and
worship songs of all time.
ISBN   1-59145-088-8

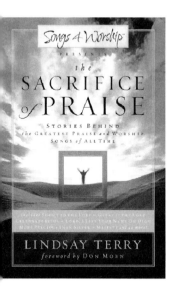

An inspiring
companion volume,
The Sacrifice of Praise
tells the fascinating stories behind
many of today's most popular
praise and worship songs.
ISBN   1-59145-014-4

INTEGRITY
PUBLISHERS

Available wherever books are sold.